PRAISE FOR

DENTAL WEALTH NATION™

"I was first impressed with Tim primarily because of his kind, caring attitude and the time he spends working with the doctors that I referred to him. I would encourage you to get your copy of Dental Wealth Nation today."

Dr. Bill Kimball | Co-Founder of Integrity Practice Sales

"I help families prepare their heirs for a successful wealth transition by assisting them in creating a legacy family plan. I do what I do because my parents passed away, and even though they had a plan, we weren't prepared. In less than nine months, I had to raise $1.8 million to pay an IRS tax bill. During this process, I discovered that less than 10% of families could retain wealth past the third generation. I also found the virtual family office, which Tim McNeely offers, and that even Tim McNeely exists. He is such a fabulous estate and tax planning strategist. He's gathered a team of experts, myself included, to support the families he serves. That's why I'm so excited about Tim's new book. Get several copies, give yourself one, and then share them with your friends. While it's too late for my mom and dad, it's not too late for you."

Cindy Arledge | Founder & CEO of Legacy Family Revolution

"Tim has established an enviable reputation as a great presenter and educator of dentists on issues never taught in dental school."

Jason Schneller | Director of Business Development at Provide, Inc.

"Tim is knowledgeable, genuine, easy to work with, and eager to assist our members in any way he can."

Lee Adishian, RDH | Executive Director of SGVDS

"Tim gives a great perspective on planning. He presents ideas with an optimistic and hopeful outlook that dentists can benefit from."

Scott Stewart | President of Clifton & Associates, Inc.

"Tim has been a reliable, honest, and thoroughly knowledgeable speaker on the subject of wealth management."

Andy Ozols, MA, MBA | Past Executive Director,
San Fernando Valley Dental Society

DENTAL WEALTH NATION™

DENTAL WEALTH NATION™

7 STEPS TO DECREASE TAXES, INCREASE IMPACT AND LEAVE YOUR THRIVING LEGACY

TIMOTHY MCNEELY
#1 BEST-SELLING AUTHOR

EXPERT AUTHORITY EFFECT™
PUBLISHING
Detroit

Dedication

JESUS CHRIST

Who suffered once for sins,
the righteous for the unrighteous,
that He might bring us to God.

DR. DANA YEOMAN

My lovely wife.
You are a gift from God.
It is a blessing to live life with you.

MY FAMILY & GRANDPARENTS

Thank you for your love and support.

MY VIRTUAL FAMILY OFFICE

You are among the best of the best.
I count it an honor to call you colleagues and friends.

DENTAL WEALTH NATION GUESTS

Thank you for sharing your knowledge with me
and for helping dentists build even more amazing lives of
significance.

MY CLIENTS AND POTENTIAL CLIENTS

Thank you for the privilege of helping you thrive
in the midst of an uncertain world.

DOWNLOAD THE AUDIOBOOK!

As a way to say *"Thanks"* for investing in my book and your thriving future, I would like to give you the professionally recorded studio version of my audiobook 100% complimentary

TO DOWNLOAD GO TO

www.DentalWealthNationBook.com/DWNAudioBonus

Contents

Foreword

by Andrew Phillips

Allow me to be transparent in revealing *my personal truth* and my life story, detailing the good, the bad, and the ugly. It is my sincerest prayer that my ups and downs inspire you to thrive in the midst of an uncertain world. Sit back and indulge in the adventure of my trials, turns, and triumphs.

First, I want to introduce you to Tim McNeely's business, **The LifeStone Companies,** where Tim excels at helping dental entrepreneurs optimize their financial world. This book provides exceptional insight and detail in a lighthearted and easy-to-understand format. In these pages, not only will you learn what it takes to achieve true success, you'll be equipped to take the necessary steps that will benefit everyone you care for the most *and* leave your thriving legacy by optimizing your financial world.

Every day in my work at The Phillips Group, I work with successful entrepreneurial dental practice owners like you, helping them make sense of their finances and eliminate their fears surrounding money so they can stay focused on their practice, which means giving their patients the best care.

In these pages, Tim takes you through multiple scenarios in the lives of characters: Dr. Virtual Family Office, Dr. Middle of Career, Dr. Exit, and Dr. Do It Yourself. Their stories will relate to your personal experiences in some way (now or in the future). Pay attention to how Tim guided them so you, too, can decrease taxes, increase impact, and leave your thriving legacy as a successful dental entrepreneur, fueling the future growth and prosperity of America.

Success, for most people, is generally measured by the attainment of money. While one's financial status is an easy measurement, I have a feeling that success for you is much more than that and includes increasing your impact and leaving your thriving legacy to your future generations as they become the sons, husbands, fathers, daughters, wives, mothers, partners, and community members preserving everything you'll be passing down.

The strategies of the super-rich and ultra-wealthy that are revealed in this book are the best of the best I have seen to help successful dental entrepreneurs like yourself optimize your financial world even more. I firmly believe that you will put yourself in the best possible position by implementing the strategies Tim shares.

I am very passionate about tax planning and the strategies you are about to discover in **Dental Wealth Nation.** To understand why, I'd like to share my personal history with you. My enthusiasm to help you optimize your financial world is a direct result of my experience, including the tragedies and the triumphs.

First off, this will not be another sob story, but I want you to know that every word comes from a heart of service. It is my sincerest intent to share deeper insights with you so that you can use them as guided inspiration throughout your journey.

It was an interesting start, to say the least . . .

I grew up in Orange County, California. My dad frequently put in long hours as a CPA, and my mom was a homemaker. Thanks to them, I enjoyed a blessed and comfortable youth. However, I was told I was a handful as a kid. Because of my exposure to a variety of environments throughout my public school years, I saw and experienced various family lifestyles. The diversity among my classmates made me realize that not all kids were as fortunate as I was. Combined with my involvement in the church, it gave me a comprehensive worldview.

My father was always eager to grow both personally and professionally throughout his CPA career. That, I believe, is a powerful asset. He was the greatest business mentor I could have wished for.

6

My grandparents were also powerful factors in my life throughout my somewhat rebellious upbringing.

My grandfather, Lou, included me in many of his church and business activities. While my grandmothers, Beverly and Helen, helped polish off those rough edges.

Grandma Helen showed me tough love with a little smack and hug, giving me the kick in the rear I sometimes needed. Grandma Beverly took a softer approach, sitting me down and teaching me life and lessons from the Bible while we baked pies together.

Despite their stark differences, I wouldn't have had it any other way. As a result, I'm a fantastic baker with a strong sense of duty and unwavering family loyalty. *You really should try my Snickerdoodles and killer boysenberry pie!*

Every year, my brother, cousins, and I gathered oranges from Grandma Beverly's orange tree. Then we'd reach over the fence with our orange-picking poles and steal more from the neighbors!

I wasn't always a mischievous kid though! Remember your childhood lemonade stands? My lemonade was made with the lemons from Grandma Beverly's plentiful tree. On this side of the fence—*literally*, I appreciated serving something that people could enjoy.

The budding entrepreneur in me relished those wonderful days.

To this day, I am unable to pass a child's lemonade stand without indulging. I know that many can't say this, but I had a wonderful childhood. I recognize how fortunate I am to have a safe and enjoyable upbringing.

Whether it was stealing oranges, skipping class, or playing pranks on friends, these events shaped me into the person I am now, and I have no regrets. What my experiences also provided was *the opportunity to decide what side of the fence I wanted to live on for the rest of my life.*

Throughout my teen and college years, a series of unfortunate events significantly impacted me. When my parents divorced and my grandparents, Lou and Beverly, developed dementia, it helped me realize how important my family was to me.

Today, you are reading words of wisdom from my personal and business life. As much as I enjoyed those early entrepreneurial experiences, I didn't always want to be in business for myself.

Originally, I had my eyes set on the military, where I could have a career over twenty years, get my pension, and at a young age, move on to other work—such as something in the private sector.

I specifically desired to join the Navy as a corpsman. Discovering I might be trapped in a submarine, I quickly determined I wanted none of that!

The Army, I learned, would be better suited for me, so I joined as a medic after high school. I wanted to serve people in a unique way. As a medic, I could serve my country while also aiding people, which I enjoyed.

I used to think seeing both sides of the tracks at a young age was what influenced my decision to enlist in the military. However, now I can say—after digging deeper—what really drew me in was my desire for selflessness, patriotism, and camaraderie.

My time in the church and serving in the military shaped many of the values I hold today. Unfortunately, it wasn't long before I was unexpectedly medically discharged from a training accident and I learned something profound:

Sometimes God closes one door so that He can open a bigger and better one for our future.

Without those doors being closed, and new ones opening, I wouldn't be where I am now.

After being medically discharged from the Army in my early twenties, I worked on ambulances, a lumberyard, and even started a dental events company. All of these experiences got me thinking:

- What are the skills I'm naturally good at?
- What do I enjoy doing the most?
- How can I best utilize my skill set?

The series of events that turned my life around...

During this same time period, my father offered me an administrative assistant job in accounting. My grandfather Lou was always encouraging me to get into the accounting field. He wanted me to follow in my father's footsteps because he saw how well my father had done for the family and himself. My father taught me a lot about business and money, which is another reason why I stayed.

Assisting my father's clients struck me as an excellent way to help others. His was a solid company that served as a vehicle to simultaneously help people in business at an honest price while making good money in return.

Little did I know that the job opportunity provided by my father would be one of the stepping stones that would lead me to where I am today. As my time with the company (and my father) progressed, I came to deeply know that success is not just a finesse of *business skills*; it's a finesse of *people skills*. I realized I didn't need to be a CPA like my father; instead, I could help people another way.

I spent many years refining my skills. Today, I am grateful to spend my days doing what I love—building and nurturing relationships, then leveraging those relationships to develop new business. I have my father to thank for this strong foundational model because I watched him grow one of the largest, most well-respected powerhouse dental CPA firms in California from the ground up.

What I learned from my father helped me strengthen my identity and establish the three core pillars on which my company now operates. My father's legacy has since been passed down through the generations. Those core pillars are on my desk, and I think about them frequently as I further develop my business.

Few professionals get to say they actually *enjoy* what they do.

I can proudly and happily share that helping people *is* my passion.

I love hearing the success stories of passion and drive from our clients. It's so rewarding to serve them while providing a fulfilling life for my family. It's a win-win for everyone because this is what my wife and I love doing every day.

Credentials are important when looking for the right partners to help you expand and maximize your business, but don't you want to know what kind of person they are? After all, you can't trust just anyone! Don't you want to know who you'll be working with as you navigate and plan major life decisions? In today's "virtual everything" society, it's crucial to find a person who is personable and integrous. Something that my team and I look for—as Tim describes—is the *human element*. What value does the company place on our relationship?

We actively seek to partner with *wholesome* businesses. The desire to assist others stems not only from my own experiences but also from who and what I aspire to be. I'm excited to be a part of this impactful book and to help you optimize your financial world past what you can even dream of. Tim's business is wholesome.

What excites me most about my profession is helping people achieve success. Everyone's success manifests differently and to different degrees. Watching the progress and journey of each person's story is uplifting and deeply affirms that I'm in the right business.

I have a dedicated team in place that can get the results our clients desire. We go above and beyond what the majority of professionals out there are doing. How do we do that? It comes back down to our three core pillars I eluded to earlier:

- We Are Innovative.
- We Are Compassionate.
- We Are Client-Focused.

The dedication to each of the pillars separately is what makes us stand above the rest in our ability to serve our clients. This is one of the reasons I believe Tim chose me to write this foreword for you.

I've experienced the lows of being medically discharged, to the highs of finding my purpose of serving others through relationship-building in the financial world. During the expansive season while working for my father, the benefits I received were life-changing. That season is also when I met my wife, Laura. It took a few attempts to persuade her I was the one, but we eventually started dating and after some time got engaged. I'm excited to say that we've been happily married since 2014.

Just when you think it's going well . . .

When life is going well, it's easy to go into auto-pilot mode. But it's during these times we often don't appreciate those who have had a significant impact on our decisions. Those who have brought us to where we are today. I can name one person in particular who positively impacted me from the start: my dear friend and cousin, Harrison. He was an active and happy kid who lived life fearlessly and fully.

Unfortunately, Harrison died too young after a motorcycle accident in 2017. His charm, passion, and resolve to live without fear lives on in many of the people he knew and influenced. He left a legacy that will live on in people's hearts forever. We both enjoyed riding motorcycles. He inspired me to never give up on what I love because of the energy and attitude he left behind. So I'm still riding. That's what he'd want.

Who is the person who has inspired you? Who has modeled for you living your life with passion?

Why is *right now* the best time in history to optimize?

I worked for my father for about eleven years before Laura and I folded his company's assets into The Phillips Group. Here, I get to feature one of my skill sets: connecting with my clients. Connection is essential to all relationships–business, spouse, children, and friends.

My connection with my team is just as important as my connection with my client. Starbucks, for example, could not have existed without what they call their *partners*. Success leaves clues. Why repeat their errors if we can learn from them what didn't work?

I have found other successful entrepreneurs to be some of my best teachers and role models. Authors, show hosts, and industry thought leaders provide valuable insight and demand for their products to serve their clients at the highest level.

We serve our clients in various ways, but our primary focus is on Full-Service Accounting, Tax Planning & Preparation, and Practice Management Consulting.

Full-Service Accounting

Not only do we balance your books and reconcile your accounts, but we do your accounting and track your expenses as a percentage of your overhead. We use those figures to benchmark your practice against your competitors and to provide you with a comprehensive, visually-appealing, and easy-to-read packet of financial statements each month.

Tax Planning & Preparation

Let's face it: taxes are a part of life, and they aren't going away anytime soon. We help clients pay taxes when they need to (such as when they are looking to buy or refinance a home) and avoid paying unnecessary taxes by strategizing ways to mitigate costs.

Practice Management Consulting

Because we utilize process automation and artificial intelligence to reduce the time-consuming data entry aspect of our job, we can spend that freed-up time helping you better understand how your practice stacks up against your competitors. We'll ask questions like, "Are you paying your dental hygienists too much or too little?" and "Why can't you hire reliable dental hygienists?"

The most surprising aspect of running this firm is that our clients want to talk to a human who cares. They want us to listen to the business, family, and financial concerns that keep them awake at night. By listening and assisting them in brainstorming a solution, even if it does not involve traditional tax planning or accounting, they can put their trust in our team and process for the best financial result.

In addition to the expertise that Tim and I provide, you might be wondering what it takes. Surprisingly, it's easier than you might think.

All you really need is patience and your willingness to understand the effort and research it could take to reach a solution.

Some clients want us to put out the fire even though they're constantly adding wood. But it's critical that if you're willing to invest your own money into some of these plans that are put in place, you have to do your part as well willingly.

When I lead our clients through our process, we revisit those core pillars and why they are so vital to your present and prospective clients. The beauty is how complementary they are with Tim's services. But both are critical components to optimizing your financial world.

You found who you need in the author of this book. Tim lays out the proactive steps you should take to help guide the needle in the right direction.

For example, I find it so important for business owners to build their personal wealth outside of their business by using the advanced strategies you'll read throughout this book, such as Advanced Planning, Donor Advised Funds, and the Virtual Family Office, to name a few. Robert Kiyosaki really said it best.

> *"The rich DON'T work for money.* **They make their money work for THEM.** *Rich people grow up knowing that wealth comes not from work, but from LEVERAGE. They invest their money and the investment vehicles do all the 'work.' "*

~ Robert Kiyosaki

Tim exemplifies this through and through with his expertise, mentoring, and genuine care. The goal of accumulating wealth outside of your business is to ensure longevity, comfort, and peace of mind. When something happens to your basket, all your eggs won't be in it, which protects your financial future and creates lasting legacy.

If you get nothing else from reading this, I want you to realize you don't have to be a billionaire to optimize your financial world.

Read that again.

> *You don't have to be a billionaire to optimize your financial world.*

Realize that the tactics of the super-rich apply to everyone—*even if this is the first time you're hearing about them.* You simply have to know how to understand them and enact them in your own life, and Tim is here to guide you.

As you'll soon discover in this book, having the right team of people in place makes all the difference in optimizing your financial world.

I'm a huge proponent of working with a team of people where each specializes in one or two things. A strong team like Tim's operates with fluidity and personal connection while providing the best-customized service to clients.

I'm thankful we met back in 2017 while attending the San Gabriel Valley Dental Society event. While they had many sponsors there, Tim's stylish bowtie made him stand out. My first thought was, *This is an unusual choice for a gentleman*—at least in this decade. I also thought it showed a uniqueness of character and personality.

Tim also struck me as a friendly professional who wasn't overly serious about himself. As our conversations progressed, we discovered that we had a lot in common as we both enjoy fine whiskey, a good round of golf, and providing excellent service to our clients with passion. I now consider him a good friend.

Tim's compassion is what I admire the most in him. As you continue to read this book, you'll feel it, too, and realize he's the "real deal." Nowadays, the real deal is a rarity.

Tim runs his business with a spirit of genuineness and his client's priorities in mind while simultaneously being appropriately vulnerable, transparent, and personable—a consummate entrepreneur. **By now, I'm sure you're seeing how easy of a decision it is to recommend Tim.**

Consider the edge of a knife. I can make an edge by bashing two rocks together until one of them becomes semi-sharp. Or I can go to a Japanese knife maker who has been honing their craft for thousands of years. Arguably, they'll both have an *edge*, but one is far superior to the other. Why would I waste all my time producing a mediocre product when I can enjoyably and profitably collaborate with the master who has perfected their skill? What's the edge you want when it comes to optimizing your financial future?—*literally and figuratively.*

You now have this book in your hands to jumpstart the optimizing of your financial world—today, not five years from now! When you get in your car, you're not expecting a mishap. You never expect or desire negative events to happen. However, **WHEN** they do, you want to know that you did everything you could to protect yourself and your loved ones. Am I right?

The same reason you put your seatbelt on to protect yourself from bumps—and potholes, down the road is the same reason you want to make daily, wise financial decisions that lead you to your optimized financial world five-plus years from now. You wouldn't drive cross-country without directions and a final destination would you?

Today's environment and technology changes have been a tremendous benefit for some people. However, I think that's also to their detriment. Anyone can easily access the Internet and sign up for a quick savings program. There's nothing wrong with that. But is it really taking you to the next level? Could the easy road prevent you from enacting *real* financial movement and change for the better?

Ultimately, you want to be doing something active by working with a professional who has spent decades honing their craft, like Tim.

Remember, you really do need that sharp knife edge.

When Tim invited me to write this foreword, I was blown away. It is an honor and a privilege. I recommend him to our clients because he's the best. I wouldn't trust anyone else with his specialties. I use him myself. We could go through his CV, or I could ask him what courses he's taken recently, but none of that matters. What matters is that he's done a great job with our clients—and my family, as well as my personal nest egg. I trust Tim with my financial future, and you should too.

With a passion for your success,
Andrew Phillips
Co-Founder & Chief Growth Officer, The Phillips Group

Preface

Congratulations! You are a successful dental entrepreneur.

You most likely have achieved a certain level of financial success, perhaps opened several practice locations, and are looking to open even more. The truth is that you are among the best at what you do.

And yet, I find many dental entrepreneurs can fail to thrive by overlooking critical areas surrounding the theme of Wealth Management.

I wrote this book so that you can take advantage of the many opportunities available to you while also helping you avoid costly errors along the way.

Even if you are not a dentist, you can apply my business techniques, which offer a time-tested framework to help you decrease your taxes, increase your client impact, leave a thriving personal legacy, and so much more.

Let me start by telling you a story about how a dentist changed the trajectory of my life.

I'll never forget November 4, 2011. I was sitting with a client—my wife, actually—in San Diego, California. Instead of enjoying the beaches, the sun, and the sand, though, we were sitting in a specialist's office, waiting for the doctor to come in and confirm to my wife if she would be able to pursue a future in dentistry or not. She had been having issues with her hands, and, as you know, your hands are everything in dentistry.

Imagine how you would feel if you were sitting with the person you loved the most waiting for a rheumatologist to come in and tell them if they have a future in their chosen career. Imagine the uncertainty, the fear, and even the terror of the unknown future. Imagine enduring exhaustive years of dental school and building a practice only to be left with grief at not being able to continue building a successful career. However, the reason I'll never forget that day is not because of the anxiety and fear we faced. I will never forget that day because it did not matter what the diagnosis was. Why?

Together, we had run the numbers and done the planning. As a result, my wife knew she would be financially okay—regardless of the outcome.

My wife was able to thrive in the midst of this uncertain future with quiet confidence because of the wealth planning we had done in advance.

Until November 2011, my career as a financial advisor had not always made an impact like it did on that day with my wife. Wealth Management ought to make a real, meaningful, and tangible difference in people's lives. And my dear wife, Dr. Dana Yeoman, is why I am now exceedingly passionate about helping dentists like you make even smarter choices with your money.

When my wife and I first started dating, I thought Wealth Management was simply managing an investment portfolio or making referrals to a professional who could help my clients out in other areas of their financial lives.

However, when I met my wife, Dana, it didn't matter how well I could manage an investment portfolio or the fact that I could call a banker and make a referral for her. The work I was doing didn't make any difference in her practice or her life. Imagine eating dinner at an elegant restaurant or taking a walk around the neighborhood when the other "boyfriend" (aka her dental practice) would unexpectedly show up and ruin the night.

You know firsthand what running a dental practice is like. The issues that would invade our time together are common for many practices. They ranged from my wife having to hold back her paycheck in order to make payroll, to being concerned about peer review with a grumpy patient, to being worried about firing an employee appropriately so they wouldn't file a complaint to the labor board.

Her dental practice was a significant source of stress. Sadly, as an ordinary financial advisor focused mainly on investments, I couldn't help Dana solve her most pressing challenges. I felt helpless and frustrated at not being able to help the person I loved the most. I also realized the way I was doing my job was all wrong, and I was increasingly dissatisfied with the impact I was not making in the lives of people financially. I knew I could take what I had learned and focus it in a more intentional way. A way that included both service and skill. I knew something had to change in a big way, but I was up for the challenge.

So I reached out and hired the best of the best in my industry to teach me what Elite Wealth Advisors are doing to help their clients accelerate their success. How do advisors serving the Ultra-Wealthy (net worth of +500 million dollars or more) do that? What are my best-of-the-best peers doing to move the needle for their clients? As I started collaborating and building a world-class team, something incredible happened. Dana and I started implementing these lessons we learned. Soon, we got back to being on top of the world. We hired the right consultant for her practice, found the right CPA, and built a fantastic team of people to support her practice. Things were smooth sailing.

What I did not know at the time was that I was building what the Ultra-Wealthy call a Virtual Family Office. I was assembling the best of the best team to help with whatever a client might require. I will dive deep into family offices in Chapter 7.

The most significant benefit of building this Virtual Family Office is that it allowed my wife and I to get back to enjoying our date nights together. The world was our oyster again.

However, life will often throw you a curveball, something you aren't ready to tackle. It may be the loss of a key employee, an unexpected tax bill, a global pandemic, or the Spanish Inquisition. (That last one was for my Monty Python fans because basically *no one* expects the Spanish Inquisition!) Or in my wife's case, the surprise was the crippling pain in her hands.

Imagine being a dentist and you lose your ability to hold forceps, making extractions impossible. As you know, hands are the lifeblood of your practice, and this was looking like a total catastrophe. We are people of faith, so we spent some time in prayer.

Once we had our heads on straight, we implemented another lesson from the Ultra-Wealthy. We ran a stress test of our plans and discovered that the well-meaning advisor who had sold my wife a disability policy straight out of dental school had advised her to set it up in a way that was detrimental to her. He is what I call a Pretender. He meant well, but he set her up for failure.

The Pretender advisor was a nice guy who wanted to help people, but he didn't have the technical skills to understand what he was recommending. He thought he was clever by making it so that my wife could pay for the policy through her business and get a tax write-off.

Sounds like a great idea to you, doesn't it? Don't you want a tax write-off?

This fellow missed explaining to my wife that if she ever required the benefits from that policy, her income would be fully taxable. The tax deduction was taken initially, but the government would take their share when she became most vulnerable.

Ouch! It was painful!

However, having discovered the error, we began paying for the policy in a way that created tax-free income later should the worst happen. We breathed a massive sigh of relief because we knew that by making a singular change, she would have the income she needed if she couldn't practice dentistry anymore.

I'll never forget sitting in the specialist's office with my wife because the sense of peace for the future was overwhelming. We knew beyond all doubt that even if she never produced another dollar in her practice, she was going to be more than okay financially.

In those moments with my wife, this job that I once hated suddenly became a passion for me. Today, I wake up excited to help dental professionals, just like you, take advantage of all the financial opportunities out there to ensure you are protected when things don't go as planned.

Dana has reached a point in her practice where she is happy and cheerful, floating along in what we call her "Dana Boat." She's moving at her speed, doing her thing, and finally pleased with her financial creation. And seeing her achieve her dreams makes me even happier.

To get a picture of what this Dana Boat looks like, I'd like you to imagine one of those silly little swan boats with foot paddles, be-bopping around a picturesque lake.

As she's paddling along in her boat, doing her happy thing, a big, red speedboat suddenly goes blazing past. My wife is very content in her little swan boat with the paddles. She nods to the speedboat and braces for the wake, but she's not even remotely envious of the responsibilities that come with the ownership of that high-performance machine.

Some of you want to be in that speedboat, which is okay. There are no right or wrong goals; your life is 100 percent personal to your desires and efforts. Dana is happy with her swan boat, but perhaps you want more.

This book is for those of you who are in the speedboat.

You own your practice.

You are a dental entrepreneur.

You are driven for *even more in life:* more patients, more locations, more success, and even more impact.

This is a book for those who want more, those who have reached a certain level of success and are craving to keep pushing even further.

This book is written to help you thrive.

As you continue to read, I will take you through all the steps in my Wealth Management Process with some fun (and revealing!) stories from the journeys of four characters:

Dr. Do It Yourself: These are the dentists I have spoken with or consulted with who have chosen to implement strategies on their own.

Dr. Middle of Your Career: These are the dentists who are at the middle point of their career, and looking to maximize their net worth.

Dr. Exit: These dentists are working on an exit plan as they look forward to their next phase in life.

Dr. Virtual Family Office: These are the dentists I have worked with who have embraced the Virtual Family Office Model.

The characters are all inspired by real-life clients whose specific details have been changed. In doing so, I can protect my client's privacy and precise information.

By the end of this book, you will be able to optimize your financial world so that no matter what life throws at you, you will be empowered to say, "I've got an amazing team of people. They have done the planning for me and have run the numbers, so I know I will be okay. I know I can thrive In the midst of this uncertain world!"

Prologue

Welcome to Dental Wealth Nation™. I'm excited to walk you through my time-tested process so you can throw yourself into the midst of an abundant world by optimizing your finances to the maximum. No matter where you currently are in life, I want you to imagine your financial future for the next quarter, the next year, and the next decade. Now imagine being able to make some minor changes today that will lead to significant results in your future.

That's how you will benefit from this process. Start small, then reap big rewards.

So grab a pen, a drink, and a snack as we explore the elements of Wealth Management and how adopting the principles in this book can help you *decrease taxes, increase impact, leave your thriving legacy*, and so much more.

There are 7 Steps to Wealth Management I've found to be the most effective, and in the following chapters, we will address each step in detail. But first I'd like to share a formula that will help unlock and unite various parts of your financial life.

Despite theoretical physicist and cosmologist Stephen Hawking's warning that *"each math equation included in a book would cut the sales in half,"* I will include just one fundamental equation: The Wealth Management Formula.

$$Wealth\ Management =$$
$$Investment\ Consulting + Advanced\ Planning + Relationship\ Management$$

This is one equation that you'll easily remember because it holds the substance and power to work in your favor if understood correctly. Let me give you a brief overview before diving deeper into each element of Wealth Management.

- Investment Consulting addresses the top concern of affluent dental entrepreneurs: preserving wealth. This also happens to be the primary offering of most financial advisors.

- Advanced Planning addresses four key areas that fall beyond the realm of investment consulting: wealth enhancement, wealth transfer, wealth protection, and charitable gifting.

- Relationship Management is made up of two parts. The first part is your advisors working with you over time through a consultative process so they can understand what matters most to you. Second, it involves the management of other professional advisors in your life to address your advanced planning concerns.

The Wealth Management Formula combined with the elements of a Virtual Family Office—*more on Family Offices later*—will enable you to achieve something that few driven dental entrepreneurs can. It will provide a framework for making informed and intelligent decisions about your wealth. This *process will also help you* maximize the probability of achieving all that is important to you, allowing you to thrive.

I can't wait to share how all of this fits together and how you can accelerate your success and reach untapped potential!

~ Timothy James McNeely

Investment Consulting

Chapter 1

*"It's not about how much you make.
It's about how much you don't lose."*

If your financial advisor has ever shown you a pie chart or talked about the importance of asset allocation, you have already seen firsthand the breadth of Investment Consulting. Investment Consulting addresses the top concern of affluent dentists: preserving wealth. It is also the primary offering of *most* financial advisors.

Investment Consulting will help you achieve your goals, such as decreasing taxes, increasing impact, and leaving your lasting legacy. But it is only one of seven elements that constitute the full spectrum of Wealth Management.

Wealth Management is one of the most overused phrases you will hear tossed around these days in the financial planning industry, and consultants try to substitute the full spectrum of its value by focusing on the single element of Investment Consulting.

By now you may be wondering, *What is the difference between Investment Consulting and Wealth Management?*

What Is Wealth Management?

If you ask ten ordinary wealth managers to define Wealth Management, you will probably receive fifteen different answers. While you are sure to receive descriptions that differ, you will likely find that their answers ultimately describe the same thing: Investment Consulting.

In fact, I'd like you to consider asking *your* current advisor, *"What is Wealth Management?"*

Investment Consulting sounds vague, but it revolves around making intelligent investment decisions that help you grow and preserve your wealth. You will most likely be shown a pie chart or two, hear something about managing your risk, and maybe—*if you are lucky*—they'll speak of the importance of aligning your investment choices with your goals. Sometimes advisors even like to toss in amorphous terms like *holistic, comprehensive planning*, and—my favorite—*seeing the big picture.*

Don't get me wrong, Investment Consulting is the cornerstone of Wealth Management, but Investment Consulting is **NOT** Wealth Management.

World's Most Accurate Pie Chart

Pie I have Eaten   Pie I have not yet Eaten

In the Prologue, I introduced you to the one and only math equation presented in this book. For the half of you who are still with me (inside nerd joke from the Prologue), let me restate The Wealth Management Formula:

Wealth Management =
Investment Consulting + Advanced Planning + Relationship Management

Sounds straightforward, but there are nuances in each step that are important for you to understand. Let me break down each one for you.

Investment Consulting

This is what 100 percent of financial advisors, investment consultants, and wealth managers provide. Some advisors handle investment consulting better than others, but most advisors won't tell you that investment consulting is *highly* commoditized. One of the hidden secrets of my industry is that most investment portfolios are very similar. While there are differences between them, they are small and subtle. In reality, most investment advisors have very similar strategies. It is much harder to make a dent in your financial universe if the focus is mainly on your investment portfolio.

Advanced Planning

This stage addresses four key areas that fall beyond investment consulting: first) wealth enhancement, second) wealth transfer, third) wealth protection, and fourth) charitable gifting.

Relationship Management

Relationship Management consists of two parts. The first part is a specific process of your advisors working with you so they can thoroughly understand what matters most to you. The second part involves the management of additional professional advisors in your life (CPAs, Property and Casualty Insurance Agents, Estate Planning Attorneys, and Life Insurance Agents, just to name a few) to help address your Advanced Planning concerns.

Now that you know the elements of the Wealth Management Formula, let's look at a simple example that illustrates the importance of Investment Consulting and shows how Advanced Planning can have an enhanced impact on your financial world. Take charitable gifting, for instance (see Chapter 5 for more detail on this topic). This is an excellent example of how it's nearly impossible to add value through investments alone.

I'd like to introduce you to Dr. DIY (Dr. Do It Yourself). Dr. DIY would like to make a gift to his local charity through a donation of $100,000. Dr. DIY calls up his current investment advisor and asks the advisor to sell off $100,000 of his current portfolio to make the gift. The advisor looks at the investment portfolio and suggests some investments to sell based on the current economic, political, and social climate.

Seems pretty simple, right? Well, not so fast. There is a slight problem called *taxes*.

Dr. DIY overlooked the fact that by selling off part of his investment portfolio, he may now be subject to capital gains taxes, which means he would **owe** taxes on his charitable gift. Suddenly, it feels as if Dr. DIY is getting punished for doing a good thing!

Had Dr. DIY been working with a wealth manager or his own Virtual Family Office (more on VFOs in chapter 3), his team would have also focused on Wealth Enhancement and the mitigation of taxes. They would have advised him not to sell the stock but instead to make a gift of the stock directly to the local charity. He would get the complete tax write-off for the donation, and Dr. DIY would not owe capital gains taxes. Neither would his chosen charity owe taxes on the gift. Therefore, they both could benefit from Dr. DIY's generosity.

That is why I say 100 percent of wealth managers and 100 percent of financial advisors offer Investment Consulting. But most of them only provide bare-bones information and often fail to place their client's best interests at the forefront while claiming to offer true Wealth Management services that maximize their investments.

Of the 210,000+ wealth managers in America who want to manage your investments, only a small percentage of these professionals are actually engaged in and are knowledgeable of true wealth management.

Take the last example above on charitable gifting. One of my favorite ways to help clients impact the causes that matter to them is called a Donor-Advised Fund (more of this excellent wealth management strategy to come in Chapter 5 on charitable gifting).

AES Nation, a nationally respected research firm on the needs and concerns of affluent business owners, discovered that nearly 60 percent of financial advisors know about Donor-Advised Funds. That means that four out of ten wealth managers do not understand what a Donor-Advised Fund is.

Let's take it a step further.

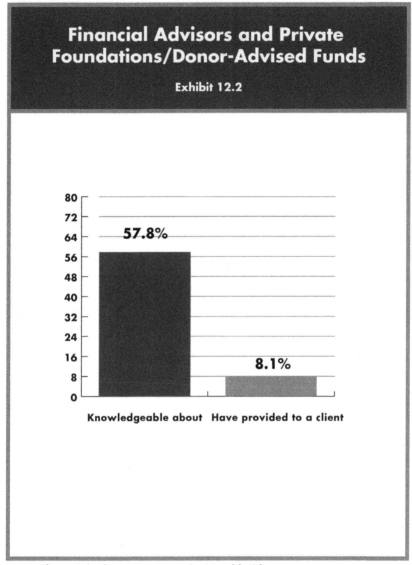

N=803 financial advisors, Source: CEG WorldWide.

Watch what happens when the AES Nation asks those same advisors, **"Have you ever implemented a Donor-Advised Fund for one client?"**

Now that number drops from almost 60 percent to 8 percent! *This means that not even one in ten wealth managers have implemented a Donor-Advised Fund for one client, even though they know about Donor-Advised Funds.*

I have personally implemented many Donor-Advised Funds for my clients and, in the process, helped them reduce their taxes and support causes they are passionate about.

You may be thinking, **Why do most advisors know things that can help their clients but never act on that knowledge?**

Good question! One of the reasons the numbers are so low is that there are many people in the financial industry whom I call **Pretenders** (more to come on Pretenders, Predators, and Elite Wealth Managers in Chapter 7).

A Pretender is a well-meaning advisor who has your best interests at heart. They want to help you. They truly do. But when it comes to knowing and implementing advanced-planning strategies, they simply don't have the technical expertise to assemble and manage a team of top-tier talent to make it happen. As a result of their limited capabilities, you get less-than-stellar service.

I didn't write this book to say, *"Look at me! I'm leaps and bounds above my peers!"* First off, calling this category of financial advisors *peers* would denote we're in the same league. This is just the beginning of me making it abundantly clear: *I am not aligned in thought or in practice with the typical financial advisor.*

Your investments are, without a doubt, the cornerstone of your wealth. It's not just the stocks and bonds and funds that you own; it's the real estate, the crypto, or any other investments, including your dental practice, in which you've entrusted your hard-earned money. Investment Consulting and managing your assets should be the bedrock of your financial wealth management plan, and you want to make sure your investments are handled correctly.

Investment Consulting is what 100 percent of financial advisors do. Every financial advisor offers Investment Consulting in some shape, form, or fashion. As you have seen, it's also the most commoditized piece of advice that's out there. You can go online and hire a robo-advisor to build a portfolio for you at a meager cost. It is genuinely commoditized, making it much harder to add value by managing investments alone.

That is why my clients leverage the Wealth Management Formula, and I want you to leverage it too! Let's jump into the next chapter and next part of the Wealth Management Formula called Wealth Enhancement. You will continue the journey with the following characters:

Dr. Do It Yourself: This character represents the dentists I have spoken with or consulted with who have chosen to implement wealth strategies on their own.

Dr. Middle Of Your Career: This character represents the dentists working and managing their finances in the middle of their careers.

Dr. Exit: This character represents the dentists I have worked with who want to create an exit plan as they get closer to retiring from their practice.

Dr. Virtual Family Office: This character represents the dentists I have worked with who have embraced the Virtual Family Office Model.

All of the above personas are based on real-life clients whose specific details have been changed for privacy.

Adiós, Pretenders! I know this is where you stop and I get started. Feel free to give my ticket away to someone else for your next *"Free Dinner Seminar."* I will not be attending!

Hopefully, dear reader, you will feel the same way when you finish the next few chapters.

Wealth Enhancement

Chapter 2

"Your most expensive business partner is the IRS."

I magine your CPA calls you and says, *"I've got good news, and I've got bad news. The good news is you had a stellar year in your business. Congratulations! The bad news is that the IRS wants a hefty portion."* If this has happened to you, then you understand the value of *tax mitigation*.

Wealth Enhancement, the first element of Advanced Planning, is about tax mitigation and keeping more of your hard-earned money in your pocket by utilizing various legal strategies and tactics available to you as a dentist.

Mitigating income taxes is one of the most significant financial concerns of many affluent individuals and couples. Reducing estate taxes and capital gains taxes ranks high on their list of concerns. This is a tip-off that it should be important to us too.

It's no surprise that so many affluent share these tax-related concerns. Taxes can—and do—eat up a great deal of one's wealth.

Since 2012, I have been using The Wealth Management Formula as the foundation for helping my clients maximize the probability of achieving their most important financial goals. As a reminder:

Wealth Management =
Investment Consulting + Advanced Planning + Relationship Management

What Is Advanced Planning?

The second component of Wealth Management is Advanced Planning. Advanced Planning is advice that goes beyond your investment portfolio and looks at four critical areas of your financial life:

- **Wealth Enhancement**: focuses on improving your cash flow and tax mitigation strategies

- **Wealth Protection:** focuses on protecting everything you have worked so hard for from being unjustly taken

- **Wealth Transfer:** focuses on passing your money and assets to the next generation

- **Charitable Gifting:** focuses on helping to support the causes you are passionate about

In the last chapter, I shared that 100 percent of investment advisors, financial advisors, and wealth managers offer Investment Consulting. However, when it comes to advisors who proactively practice Advanced Planning for their clients, that number isn't even 100 percent close. According to AES Nation, a nationally respected research firm, only 6.8 percent of financial advisors proactively provide Advanced Planning. Or, to put it another way, less than one in ten advisors proactively provide advice beyond the investment portfolio.

In the same way, an investment advisor should update your investment portfolio to reflect your changing goals. An Elite Wealth Planner—a planner with technical expertise who focuses on *discovery* and the *human element*—will update your Advanced Planning needs as your goals and plans change in each phase of life. (More about Elite Wealth Planners and the human element in Chapter 6.)

The Role of Discovery in Advanced Planning

Discovery (see Chapter 6 for more info) plays a significant role in Advanced Planning. If an advisor fails to conduct discovery, then the advisor will not understand your unique situation and will therefore be unable to help you achieve your most important personal goals.

If you don't know your goals, how can you choose the best strategies, implement the best tactics, and decide what strategy and tactics to put into place? It's like surgically placing an implant without first reading the patient's X-ray!

The Dental Wealth Nation Unlimited Discovery™ Process

My process is focused on one element. *You.* It's focused on what my mentor and coach, Russ Alan Prince, calls the *human element*. It's solely focused on your wants, desires, goals, and objectives.

For instance, if I was sitting down with you, the first thing I would ask is, *"What is important about money to you?"* I want to know what you value when it comes to money. Is it security, predictability, freedom, control, or maybe the ability to provide for your family? I want to know your goals, both financial and non-financial. After that, I want to know about the most critical relationships in your life. Once the foundations are laid, then and only then will I start to learn about your assets and liabilities.

For example, assume your dental practice is producing $23 million a year in revenue, and your biggest concern is using Wealth Enhancement to reduce your tax liability. How awkward would it feel if your financial advisor kept calling you with market updates instead of sharing a strategy that could save you one million dollars or more in taxes? That could mean you are most likely working with an investment consultant who has not engaged in discovery with you.

Discovery is crucial because if your advisors are not asking the right questions, they are missing significant opportunities to help you. If you've never had an advisor engage in discovery with you, or if it's been a while, you should schedule time to do it.

Having advisors on your team who ask you in-depth questions is easy, simple, and can be done in less than an hour. This is one of the quickest wins you can have because it will get your advisors focused on you. Simply call your existing advisor, share your goals, and ask, *"How are you helping me reach my financial goals?"* If they start asking additional questions to dive deep with you, that's a good sign. If they start talking more than listening, you may want to consider hiring another advisor.

To get the most benefit from advanced planning while harnessing the power of your own Virtual Family Office, you need to make a list of what's most important to you. Then you want to work with advisors who will help you clarify and articulate even further what drives your goals. Overall, you want advisors who are always in discovery mode with you.

Before sharing an example of the Wealth Enhancement component of Advanced Planning, I want to address some questions I always get asked.

Q: Tim, how do I know these additional strategies to mitigate my taxes are legal and safe? How do I know they will not get me in trouble?

A: *These strategies are tried and true. They are middle-of-the-road strategies that don't even get close to the red line. Your life has enough risk, and you certainly don't want to introduce additional risk if you don't have to. If you want to take advantage of strategies right down the middle road—strategies that will help maximize your net worth, help you pay the least in taxes, and keep you on the straight and narrow—you're reading the right book.*

Q: How do I know it will work for me and my unique situation?

A: *The way you know it's going to work for you and your unique circumstance all comes back to discovery and Elite Wealth Planning. Elite Wealth Planning is what the Super Rich do by working with professionals who really understand what's important to them. These Elite Wealth Planners don't approach their clients with an agenda or a product to push. They don't show up with a specific strategy they want to sell. Instead, Elite Wealth Planners ask:*

- What is important to you?
- What do you want to achieve?
- What is the legacy you want to leave?

Once you get clear on these questions, then suddenly the product, solution, and strategies become crystal clear. Why? Because you are now aligned with your goals.

Wealth Enhancement is all about getting your cash flow up and your tax bill down.

I've never met a dentist who said, *"Tim, I'd love to pay more than my fair share of taxes."* Most are willing to pay their fair share, but not a penny more.

On top of personal taxes, you're also running a business. One of the most significant expenses you're going to face time and time again is your not-so-silent business partner, Uncle Sam, who wants his cut.

There is a joke I like to make:

Q: What's the difference between tax avoidance and tax evasion?

A: *About eight inches.*

Eight inches is the typical thickness of a prison wall. Tax evasion will put you in jail, but tax avoidance will put more money in your pocket.

You never want to be involved in tax evasion. Tax evasion is absolutely illegal. It is not allowed. You are not permitted under any circumstance to evade paying taxes. If you owe taxes, you'd better pay them.

However, there's this beautiful thing called *tax avoidance*. Tax avoidance is using the tax code to legally reduce your tax liability. Tax avoidance, unlike tax evasion, is 100 percent legal. It's also supported and encouraged by the IRS!

Let that sink in for a moment. You are allowed to *avoid* taxes.

You are supposed to pursue and use all the tax breaks available to you.

Wealth Enhancement is all about making sure you never pay more than your fair share in taxes by taking advantage of the tax code that you can use. Let's focus on putting more money in your pocket and less money in the government's pocket. Doing so also allows you to give more to your loyal employees. I think you'd agree that you and your employees know how to use your money better than the government. Am I right?

Wealth Enhancement, however, is not only about mitigating taxes and getting your cash flow up. It's also about weaving all the other aspects of your financial world together.

That's why your initial discovery meeting and ongoing discovery meetings are so important. When I work with my clients, I want to know their overall goals and be responsive when their plans change.

For example, you may be interested in:

- Getting a substantial tax deduction
- Putting away money to fund your retirement
- Reducing your tax liability
- Selling your company to your employees
- Or maybe you want to pay zero in taxes?

That's easy. Give all your *money* away. Problem solved. You will pay close to nothing in taxes. However, giving all your money to charity may not be the best decision. That's why discovery is essential. Discovery is so important that it gets its own section in Chapter 6, where I elaborate and show you what good discovery looks like and give you a list of questions your advisor should be asking you.

Therefore, who you work with really makes a difference. Pretenders, Predators, and Elite Wealth Planners make a difference in Advanced Planning. Remember, less than one in ten advisors engage in Advanced Planning. That's why you want to be set up well, make sure you are protected, and know you are working with the right advisor. And by right advisor I don't mean a *single* advisor. I mean a *team* of talented people working for you.

During Regular Progress Meetings with my clients (more on this when I share the Dental Wealth Nation Wealth Management Process™ with you), the Virtual Family Office and my professional network offer input into my clients' situations. It's a multi-specialty approach with professionals from different disciplines. This allows us to weave together all the elements of wealth management in a cohesive way to maximize your results.

Let me share with you an example of how discovery can help with Wealth Enhancement and is aided by the input of a Virtual Family Office.

How Dr. VFO used Wealth Management and Virtual Family Office to Decrease Taxes, Increase Impact, and Leave a Lasting Legacy

Dr. VFO's story is a combination of actual clients I work with, but the details have been changed to protect their privacy.

I've been working with Dr. VFO for the last decade. Dr. VFO first started working with me to help optimize her company's qualified retirement plan. By working together with top-of-the-line retirement plan experts, we generated around $75,000 a year of tax savings using specialized Wealth Enhancement strategies of a 401(k) and a Profit Sharing Plan. This allowed Dr. VFO and her spouse, who also happens to be a dentist, to save substantial sums for their retirement, reward their employees, and generate tax savings.

Along the way, I continued to engage in discovery with Dr. VFO. During discovery, it came up that while she and her husband had a substantial net worth, their assets were at risk (Wealth Protection) because they had never planned for long-term care. Long-term care can be very expensive. Members of my own family are paying close to $15,000 a month for assisted living—in a small town! It can be an astronomical cost. This was an issue we discovered and helped to proactively address for them.

As Dr. VFO and her spouse prepared to sell their dental practice and retire, I brought in one of the best practice sales advisors to help with their transition. They were able to get the full asking price for their practice. Sounds great, right?

Well, yes, it was pretty great. However, the IRS, their not-so-silent partner, demanded to be paid. My clients will owe close to $500,000 in taxes from the sale of their practice.

Back to discovery. I started asking Dr. VFO and her spouse if they had rethought what charities and causes were important to them. They had always been charitably inclined but liked to make little gifts to charity as things came up. When I asked about what was important to them this time around, their answer differed significantly.

They shared they had a love for the arts and always wanted to help support a local art foundation. However, due to their busy work life, they could never participate in all the events the local art foundation put on.

So I continued the discovery process by asking more questions. How much would Dr. VFO like to give? Why did they want to donate? What were their intentions with this local charity?

As I continued to dive deep, Dr. VFO shared that her mother had played a significant role in the local community. Her mother was one of the original dreamers to settle in the area and had played an essential role in helping to make the community a much better place in its early years. The local historical society was actually in the process of building a memorial garden, and Dr. VFO wanted to help fund a memorial to her mother.

"*Would you be interested in helping fund the art foundation and helping fund the memorial garden?*" I asked.

"*We would love to!*" Dr. VFO and her husband proclaimed.

"*How would you like to give over $150,000 to these two important causes, reduce the taxes you owe on the sale of your dental practice, and have additional funds set aside for future giving?*" I asked.

"*How can we do that?*" they said in unison.

"*Wealth Enhancement is how!*" I proclaimed.

I briefly reviewed their financial plan and calculated that giving $150,000 to the local art foundation and historical society would not impact their retirement. They could financially support that kind of gift.

Next, I did a quick tax savings calculation.

"How would you like to make that gift and have it save you $75,000 in taxes?"

It made all the sense in the world.

In less than one hour, I was able to help two clients whom I love dearly give away $150,000 to help support two causes they are passionate about—*and save them $75,000 in taxes!*

Welcome to the power of Wealth Enhancement powered by discovery.

While the steps are not necessarily linear, it's a framework for providing Wealth Management. It's crucial that you look at all of these things together because if any one element is missing, then Wealth Management is not at play.

These are just a few examples of how Wealth Enhancement can benefit you. If you would like more examples, you can visit www.DentalWealthNationBook.com and get a FREE copy of *Becoming Seriously Wealthy*, which has many more examples of Wealth Enhancement.

This brings us to the second element of advanced planning called *wealth transfer,* which is all about how you can take even better care of the people you love.

Wealth Transfer

Chapter 3

*"By being proactive in your wealth transfer planning,
you can benefit your heirs and leave a lasting legacy."*

Wealth Transfer is about taking care of your heirs. It is facilitating the most tax-efficient way to pass on your assets to the people you love with minimal difficulty and cost. In order to make sure your heirs benefit to the fullest extent possible, you want to transfer your wealth in an efficient manner.

Most likely the dental industry has treated you well. As a result, you have generated significant wealth. If that's the case, you'll want to seamlessly transfer your assets to the people you love and care about and tie it all together in a way that makes sense for you while supporting your most important goals.

Transferring your wealth successfully has a meaningful impact on the people who matter most to you. In the process, you are able to make a massive benevolent dent in the universe. You know . . . the dent that allows you to help others in life-changing ways.

It's possible you may have even done some Wealth Transfer Planning already. Perhaps you have looked into education funding, helped your kids purchase their first house or property, or even created an estate plan.

Your benevolence toward your family (and even the institutions that are significant to you) drive your passion to support and care for the people and things that matter to you. This means that your motivation behind Wealth Transfer is massively important.

Estate Planning

As you know, Wealth Transfer isn't limited to giving money away to charities. It's also about transferring wealth to the next generation—namely your family and loved ones.

The statistics on estate planning are very surprising. In fact, they reveal that many dental entrepreneurs are not as ready to "transfer their wealth" as they think they are.

If I were to ask, *Do you have an estate plan?"* you most likely would say, *"Yes, I do."*

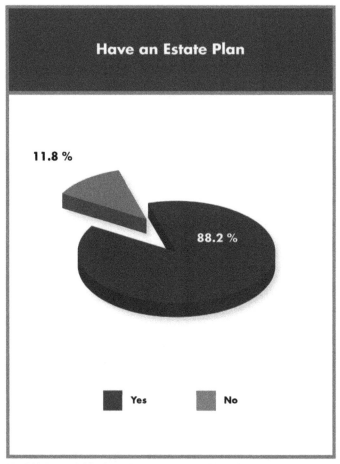

N = 262 Successful Business Owners. Source: AES Nation

In a survey out of 262 successful business owners by AES Nation, a nationally respected research firm, 88.2 percent of business owners say, *"Yes, we have an estate plan."* With 88.2 percent of business owners having an estate plan, you may be thinking this is an area that is all taken care of. However, nothing could be further from the truth.

The first thing AES Nation discovered was that 84.8 percent of current estate plans are more than five years old. At first glance, that may not seem to be a big deal. However, asking additional questions helps to illustrate what those issues are. When AES Nation asked, *"Have there been any changes since you last created your estate plan?"* we discovered the following time gaps: 62.8 percent of business owners have grown wealthier, and 76.2 percent have had a major life change. Here is why that matters for you.

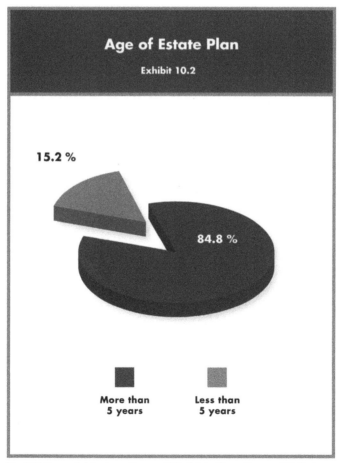

N = 231 Successful Business Owners With Estate Plans. Source: AES Nation.

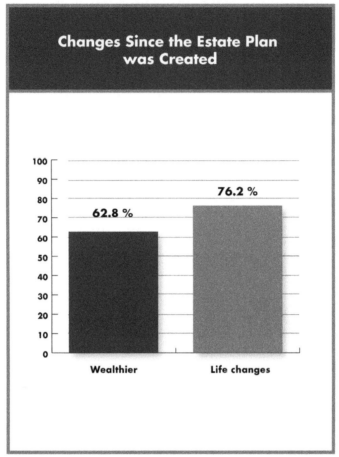

Changes Since the Estate Plan was Created

N = 231 Successful Business Owners With Estate Plans. Source: AES Nation

There have been continual changes in tax law—nationwide and statewide. Many of the older estate plans don't take advantage of the current opportunities that are available to you. Plus, additional tax law changes in the future could mean that, once again, some of those older aspects of your estate plan are not as efficient as they could be.

Your net worth has likely increased since you first made your estate plan. Your business valuation has likely increased, or maybe the ownership structure of your company has changed. Chances are, your estate plan doesn't properly reflect these changes.

Keep in mind that life is like a perpetual movie. It's not a one-time snapshot.

Five years is a good chunk of time. Perhaps you have experienced the joyous birth of a child or grandchild. Conversely, there may have been death, divorce, or something unfortunate that occurred in your family—maybe even all of the above.

The more your life has changed, the higher the chance that your estate plan is not going to be effective in accomplishing what you want it to achieve. Even though you think you are prepared, chances are you're not as prepared as you think.

Meet Dr. Exit

Dr. Exit has built an incredible successful Dental Service Organization, or DSO as they are commonly known. His DSO included twenty-two locations, thirty-four million in annual revenues, and $3.2 million in EBITDA. At an eight times valuation, he is looking at a potential valuation of $25.6 million. Dr. Exit has indeed built a very successful business. Before you start arguing with me over valuations, remember that this is a case study to help illustrate concepts that have the potential to benefit you! So please, don't send me angry tweets telling me my valuations are off! :)

Dr. Exit is sixty years old and has decided he would like to exit at some point in the near future. Dr. Exit has a Virtual Family Office and a team of advisors who ask really good questions. As I keep reminding you, everything always comes back to discovery. At this point, I can almost hear what you are thinking: *Tim, you sound like a broken record!* Yes, I know I do!

Say it with me now: discovery, discovery, discovery!

Dr. Exit's Virtual Family Office suggests he considers "freezing" the value of his DSO. This strategy has the potential to help Dr. Exit sell his DSO and maximize his personal wealth. This strategy uses a certain kind of trust to freeze the value of his business for estate tax purposes. By freezing the value of his DSO, Dr. Exit can more efficiently transfer his wealth to his loved ones when the time comes.

In *Becoming Seriously Wealthy*, we share the following example. Dr. Exit chooses to make a gift of $500,000 in stock to a grantor trust and sells another $4.5 million in company stock to the trust. If the value of his DSO increased by 10 percent annually for nine years, and then he decided to sell the company, there would be more than $2.2 million available for his family. *In the future, the trust would continue to grow, and all the appreciation would pass to the next generation without further taxation.*

Imagine passing on wealth to the next generation without it being subject to additional taxation. That's what freezing the value of your dental practice can do. However, once again, this is a strategy that advisors know about but often don't implement. What is worse is this is a major missed opportunity for a successful dentist. Only 11.1 percent of successful business owners have frozen the value of their business. Take a look at the data from AES Nation.

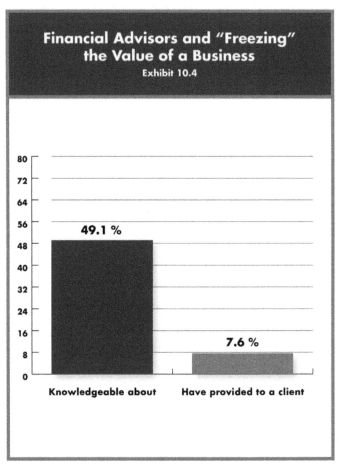

Financial Advisors and "Freezing" the Value of a Business
Exhibit 10.4

N = 803 Financial Advisors. Source: CEG Worldwide

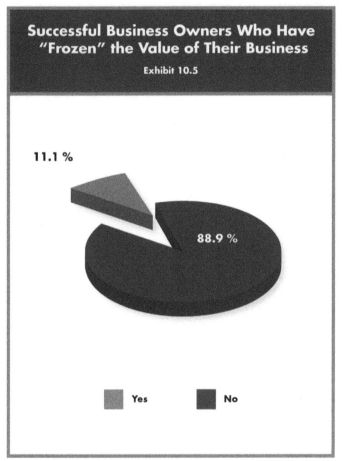

Successful Business Owners Who Have "Frozen" the Value of Their Business

Exhibit 10.5

11.1 %

88.9 %

Yes   No

N = 262 Successful Business Owners. Source: AES Nation.

The Power of Life Insurance in Wealth Transfer

When it comes to wealth transfer, life insurance can also play a major role in helping to mitigate and pay the estate taxes due on a large estate. However, life insurance is often confusing and "sold" by advisors looking for a large commission as opposed to being used as a strategy to help you achieve your most important goals.

First and foremost, when it comes to insurance, term insurance is all that is usually required. It keeps your cost low, protects the people you love, and keeps you protected while you are paying off debt. However, if you're looking for places to park excess cash flow, or if you require Estate Planning, then you may want to look at other options.

Premium Financed Life Insurance

One option that may be useful is Premium Financed Life Insurance. This strategy allows you to borrow money to help pay for life insurance that can be used to cover estate taxes. It also has the added benefit of potentially creating a self-supporting policy a couple of years down the road that can be used to generate tax-free income when you want it.

But like I have mentioned many times. Discovery is the most important element.

You want to start by looking at where you have been investing your money. The order of operations I look at for my clients is designed to help maximize tax savings. We start with maxing out a 401(k) plan. From there, we want to max out a profit-sharing plan. If additional tax savings are required, we may look at adding on a defined benefit plan or cash balance plan.

If, after all that, you still have excess cash flow, we can start looking for a captive insurance company or even life insurance as a way to create additional opportunities for saving. However, many advisors recommend reversing this order. Instead of starting with maximizing tax savings, they start by getting their clients to fund high-dollar life insurance policies where there is no immediate tax mitigation taking place.

For example, if you are paying 50 percent of your income in taxes and want to make a $100,000 contribution to your retirement plan, it will cost you $100,000 because you get to make that contribution *before* taxes. If you want to fund your life insurance policy with $100,000, it is actually going to *cost you* $200,000 because your business partner, the IRS, will ask for $100,000 in taxes.

As an example of how this can work for you, let's assume you are putting money away into your qualified retirement plan or have already accumulated a substantial amount of savings for retirement. Your advisor has pointed out that you will most likely face an estate tax issue. What can you do?

First, let's examine the benefits of Premium Financed Life Insurance. This strategy involves borrowing money from a third-party lender. At some point in the future, you will be responsible for paying back the loan with interest. What's great about this type of life insurance is that you will receive the benefits of tax-free growth of the money inside the life insurance policy. This can potentially be used to cover some or all of those costs.

Like many of the other strategies and tactics mentioned in this book, only a small number of advisors are actually aware of them, and even fewer business owners are putting these money-making opportunities into practice.

As you read this chapter, remember this: life insurance is detrimental for transferring wealth. The problem with most life insurance agents is their one-size-fits-all approach. But just like everything else, the fact pattern has to fit.

Creating wealth by having a pool of monies that you can borrow from and that generate tax-free income has to be part of your strategy. However, there is an ideal game plan for doing this. Like anything, you want to diversify, but Premium Financed Life Insurance is very unique.

How is it unique? In a nutshell, this type of insurance allows you to borrow money from the bank to purchase life insurance that can eventually cover your estate taxes. How does that sound?

Borrowing from the bank to purchase your life insurance policy enables you to acquire the policy for a lot less money than paying for it through your cash flow. What you essentially do is borrow money from a third-party lender and then, in the future, pay back that loan with interest.

Usually, that internal growth—the tax-free growth of the funds inside the life insurance policy—might cover some or all of those borrowing costs. The growth in that insurance policy, if the strategy works as intended, pays for the cost of borrowing those funds.

In addition to saving in that area, financing the premiums gives you control because you don't have to make those massive out-of-pocket premium payments because they're being made by the bank. How? You've borrowed the money to do it.

There are several ways to structure these transactions:

- Borrowing the money to pay for the premium
- Paying interest on the loan annually
- Paying the loan interest into the loan itself

Once again, there are various, powerful strategies in which to structure this, but the goal is clear: purchasing larger life insurance policies that require less cash from your personal funds, enabling you to receive money to pay estate taxes at a much lower cost.

According to AES Nation, only 41.8 percent even know about Premium Financed Life Insurance. That means six out of ten advisors have never even heard of Premium Financed Life Insurance. When it comes to implementing this strategy, only 3.5 percent of advisors have actually executed this for one of their clients. Let that sink in. Less than one out of twenty advisors have ever implemented this for one single client. What a major missed opportunity.

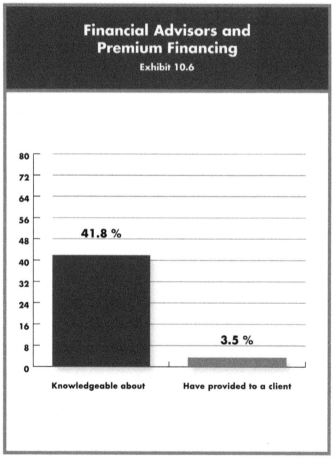

N = 803 Financial Advisors. Source: CEG Worldwide.

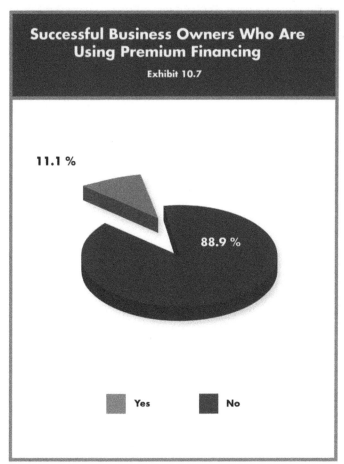

Successful Business Owners Who Are Using Premium Financing

Exhibit 10.7

11.1 %

88.9 %

Yes   No

N = 262 Successful Business Owners. Source: AES Nation.

This is also a missed opportunity among business owners, too, because research states that only 11 percent of this group (1 out of 10) have implemented premium financing. Ninety percent of the professionals don't even know about it or haven't even looked at a deal on it.

If the statistics are representative of you, then I urge you to do an insurance audit and appraisal. An appraisal will reveal what your insurance looks like.

- Do you have the right amount of coverage?
- Will the policy be self-sustaining?
- What are the long-term risks and rewards of this coverage?

In *Becoming Seriously Wealthy*, we shared the following case study. Here it is again because I find immense value in the takeaways:

CASE STUDY: Premium-Financed Life Insurance

To see how Premium Financed Life Insurance can help generate serious wealth, consider this example of a successful business owner who is forty-five years old, in excellent health, and wants $10 million of permanent life insurance.

If he were to purchase a $10 million life insurance policy, the premiums would be about $92,000 a year for the rest of his life. If he lived to be eighty-five, he would end up paying about $3.7 million for coverage.

Let's say he finances the premiums instead. In this scenario, the business owner borrows a total of about $2.6 million over five years. Meanwhile, he pays only the interest on the loan—$78,000 annually—for fifteen years. For the first five years of the policy, the business owner has to post some collateral (which, in this case, is part of his investment account). After five years, the only collateral required is the money in the policy.

After fifteen years, the loan is paid off and the life insurance policy becomes self-supporting. This means that the business owner has no more premium payments on his $10 million policy. In addition, there is now about $2 million of cash in the policy that he can access if needed. Even better, the policy's cash value is projected to grow at a greater rate than the cost of the life insurance. Thus, this business owner has secured his life insurance policy at a significant discount versus if he had made traditional premium payments.

This solution also offers the business owner an option for early payouts. He anticipates that in about twenty years he will no longer need the $10 million of coverage. If that proves to be the case, he can reduce the level of the life insurance and take money out of the policy—without having to pay any taxes on that money. In one scenario, he would be able to take out more than $230,000 a year for twenty years—effectively tax-free. *Source: AES Nation*

Corporate Pre-Sale Planning

When it comes to exiting your business, there are three big drivers that you can use to maximize the amount of money you put in your pocket: Corporate Pre-Sale Planning, Skilled Negotiation, and Wealth Management. It's time to focus on these in more detail.

One of the biggest opportunities I see (and often the one people miss out on the most) is Corporate Pre-Sale Planning. Typically, this step doesn't get done. Corporate Pre-Sale Planning requires taking time *before* you sell your company to ask yourself crucial financial questions that can make or break the successful sale of your business when it's time to exit. This is not done when you're in negotiations or two weeks before you close. Many of my clients ask, *"What exactly is Corporate Pre-Sale Planning?"* Basically, it's a strategic question-and-answer session.

- What does your exit plan look like?
- Do you have an up-to-date valuation of your dental practice?
- Have you made sure that everything is going to transfer the way you want?
- Have you worked on your numbers?"
- Have you cleaned up your finances?
- Are you clear on what you want to have happen?

Pre-Sale Planning will give you a starting point and allow you to look at where you are now and how the choices you make will impact your future. It can help you discover areas that may fail and also reveal opportunities for improvement.

Unfortunately, very few (if any) dental entrepreneurs are working with a team to help with Corporate Pre-Sale Planning. You may call your CPA, your wealth manager, or even a tax attorney to ask, *"What can I do?"* You would think that Pre-Sale Planning is commonplace; in reality, it hardly takes place.

Skilled Negotiation

The second thing that can be done to help you accelerate your success while working on wealth transfer is Skilled Negotiation. After you complete your Corporate Pre-Sale Planning, you will want to negotiate skillfully with the people who are going to purchase your business. Chester Karrass, one of the world's best negotiators, said, *"In life, you don't get what you deserve. You get what you negotiate."* The same is true when it comes to selling your business.

Premium Finance & Estate Planning

Once you're done with Corporate Pre-Sale Planning and Skilled Negotiation, your third focus should return to Wealth Management.

Wealth Management always asks you to consider: *How well do all these things fit together?* Remember, it's not about how much money you make; it's about how much money you keep. When you can keep more money in your pocket after the sale, that's the mark of a successful transaction. Hoping for the highest bid and closing on it is not necessarily the way you will end up with the most money after the sale. Sounds like a contradiction, right? Instead, you want to focus on what's going to give you the most money after everything is closed and the advisors and the IRS have been paid. This is the number that really matters. How do you arrive at this number? Again . . . strategy!

Wealth Management ties together how to invest the proceeds from the sale of your business, lower your tax bill, take care of the next generation, protect your assets, and support the causes that matter to you. Wealth Management will bring together the professionals in all areas of wealth management to help you achieve even more.

Virtual Family Office

There are numerous benefits of having a Virtual Family Office. First, it brings together top-tier talent in all the various areas of your financial life. Perhaps you have an amazing team already, or perhaps you have the start of an amazing team, or no team at all. Maybe you have some top-notch experts who can help you in one or two of those areas, but you still require top-notch experts in other areas. A Virtual Family Office is one of the best ways to achieve your desired outcome.

Again, this is why discovery is so important. Discovery will reveal what kind of team and professionals you have in place. Discovery will help you answer these questions:

- What strategies do you currently have in place?
- How do those strategies work for you Pre-Sale and Post-Sale?
- How can additional ideas and strategies be used to tie everything together in a way that's going to deliver even better results for you?

Exit Planning

Exit Planning falls under Wealth Transfer. When you sell your business, you will most likely end up with a large sum of money. The upside is you've certainly created for yourself a windfall. The downside is that it can create some tax issues and actually complicate your financial life. By creating an exit plan (and updating it periodically), you can better navigate the sale of your business and learn how to manage your profits and investments in the most savvy (and still legal!) way.

Estate planning kicks in when you sell your business for a lot of money. You're going to have some estate planning considerations to go through both before selling the business and afterward. Therefore, think about how you can best protect everything you've worked hard to build.

Once again, Wealth Management will play a key role—before and after you've sold your business. It is an important aspect throughout all stages of your career: beginning, middle, and end. Whether you're aware of it or not, you are always coordinating the various components of your financial life: investments, estate planning, asset protection, planning, and charitable gifting. So it makes sense to arrange them around your wants and needs, bringing together your coordinated team to help you achieve your desired outcome.

This is where the Exit Planning part of Wealth Management kicks in. The goal of selling should be making sure you end up with the highest after-tax dollars in your pocket. If you sell your business for $80 million and you're left with $100,000, that wasn't such a good transaction, right? The question is, "What is the after-tax net amount that you are going to walk away with?"

By working with a high-quality wealth manager prior to your sale, you can start stress testing the legal and financial strategies that you've put in place and ask questions like, "If I sell today, what does this look like? What's the outcome? What do I do once I've sold my business? How does Wealth Management play a role after my exit?"

It turns out that Wealth Management continues to play a role even after you've sold your dental business. You just had a massive liquidity event. For many of you, this will be your biggest payday ever. You will now find yourself with a significant financial windfall.

Now more than ever, you will want to look at how your assets are going to be managed post-sale. How are you going to manage not just your liquid assets but your real estate and other assets?

Some of the issues you can run into at this point are 1) outliving your wealth—it's possible you are not managing your assets in a way that is designed to preserve and grow your wealth, and 2) paying far more taxes than you should because you never took the time to integrate investment management with the other areas of Advanced Planning. These issues can lead to serious financial and legal mistakes that will be problematic economically and personally—to you and your family.

Once again, it's Wealth Management to your rescue.

A Virtual Family Office can help you bring together Investment Management, Wealth Enhancement, Wealth Transfer, Asset Protection and Charitable Gifting in a holistic way that will help you maximize the opportunity of achieving all that is important to you.

Selling the Business

So let's say you sell your business. What else is there to consider?

Asset Protection is still the key factor because the way you protect a business is different than how you protect liquid assets. How do you protect personal assets? Up until the sale, you may have been using LLCs, big umbrella policies, and all sorts of different protection strategies to protect your business. But now that your money has transferred into personal assets, you must employ different tactics and strategies to grow and protect your money via charitable trusts, Donor-Advised Funds, and employee stock ownership plans, to name a few.

The numbers don't lie; they show the missed opportunities out there for people, but *only if they plan ahead!*

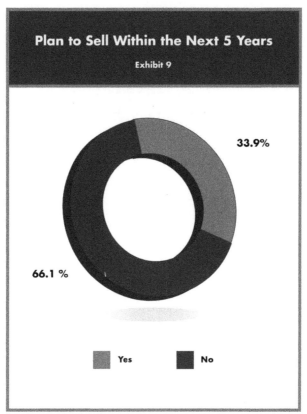

Plan to Sell Within the Next 5 Years

Exhibit 9

33.9%

66.1 %

Yes   No

Source: AES Nation, 2018. N = 616 Self-made Business Owners.

Rationale for Selling

Exhibit 10

Reason	Percentage citing reason
Expect to get a very good price	85.6%
Increasing competition	60.6%
The business is increasingly harder to run	48.6%
The industry is changing	35.6%
Want to retire	21.6%
Want to do something else in business	17.3%

Source: AES Nation, 2018. N = 208 Self-made Business Owners.

In a study conducted of 616 self-made business owners who want to sell, more than a third of them want to do so in the next five years. In another study of 208 self-made business owners, you see the top-six rationale for selling. More than 20 percent of them want to retire, and over 85 percent expect to get a very good price.

Sounds great, but when you start diving into the numbers, a different scenario emerges. If Asset Protection and Wealth Management is important to you, what have you actually done to secure your future? Do you have a formal transition plan in place?

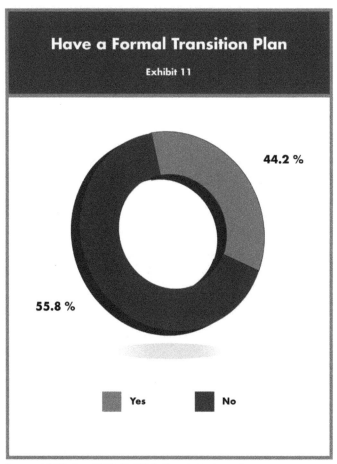

Have a Formal Transition Plan

Exhibit 11

44.2 %

55.8 %

■ Yes   ■ No

Source: AES Nation, 2018. N=208 Self-made Business Owners.

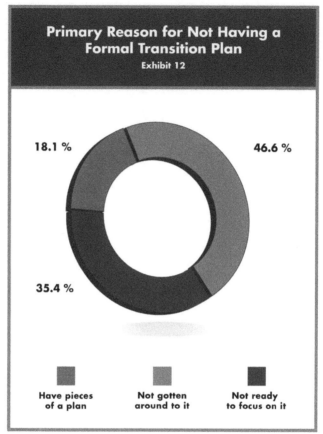

Primary Reason for Not Having a Formal Transition Plan
Exhibit 12

18.1 %

46.6 %

35.4 %

Have pieces of a plan

Not gotten around to it

Not ready to focus on it

Source: AES Nation, 2018. N = 116 Self-made Business Owners.

Fifty-five percent of business owners do not have any kind of transition plan in place. When asked why they haven't established a transition plan, here's what they had to say:

- 46 percent say they've *"not gotten around to it."*

- 35 percent say they're *"not ready to focus on it."*

- 18 percent say they *"only have pieces of the plan."*

No matter the scenario, the unfortunate outcome is the same: they haven't put the pieces together in a comprehensive way. This is a huge missed opportunity for them in terms of the planning that can be done. Most business owners aren't doing any kind of prepping. In fact, only 18 percent have done any planning, and that's only pieces of a larger plan. They haven't thought things through holistically.

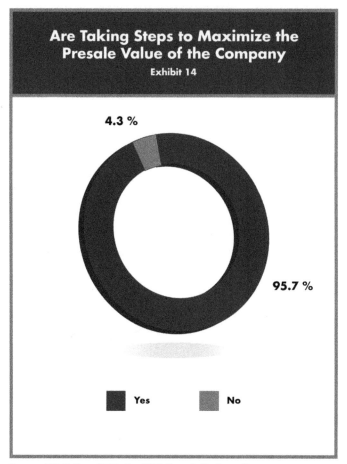

Are Taking Steps to Maximize the Presale Value of the Company

Exhibit 14

4.3 %

95.7 %

Yes   No

Source: AES Nation, 2018. N = 92 Self-made Business Owners.

The research reveals that 95.7 percent are "taking steps to maximize the presale value of the company." But what's odd is what happens after the sale...

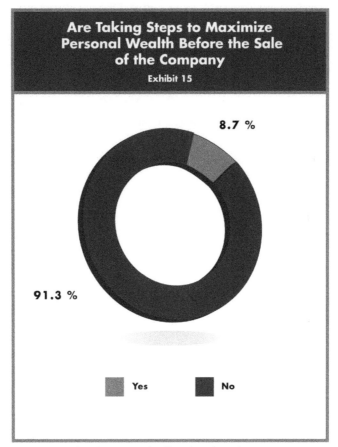

Are Taking Steps to Maximize Personal Wealth Before the Sale of the Company

Exhibit 15

8.7 %

91.3 %

Yes   No

Source: AES Nation, 2018. N = 92 Self-made Business Owners.

Suddenly, they are no longer taking steps to maximize their personal wealth before the sale of the company. They work really hard to maximize the value of their business, but when it's sold, they begin to live life on autopilot. As a result, 91 percent of those same people aren't doing anything to maximize their personal wealth.

Personal Profit vs. Profitable Company

Whether you are in that 95 percent who have actually taken steps to maximize the pre-sale value of your company, or if you are in the 91 percent who haven't taken any steps to maximize your personal wealth before the sale of your company . . . Well, you're in the majority. It's okay, but the great news is that we can now fix it—*and you won't potentially lose millions.*

What's interesting is that nearly all dental entrepreneurs plan their corporate exit. Yet a large majority do Corporate Exit Planning, and a large minority do not do Elite Wealth Planning. Why is this?

This could be due in large part to all the business coaches coming in, marketing those services. You're allowed to talk about maximizing business value with them, but all of a sudden, maximizing personal net worth is not necessarily as acceptable to them as building a highly profitable company.

Building personal wealth is a great thing to do. If you truly care about others, if you care about giving back and you've got a talent and an ability to make money, you should strive to make as much money as you can. It enables you to give more. It enables you to take care of more people. It enables you to be even more generous. Personal wealth planning is huge. You should take it just as seriously as building a profitable company because the two goals work together.

By tying these two goals together, you create a more powerful business model. Unfortunately, most aren't focused on the personal side whatsoever.

Charitable Trust or Donor-Advised Fund?

I have a chapter devoted to charitable gifting and Donor-Advised Funds. In fact, they are the last element of advanced planning. However, Wealth Management ties all these elements together. Nothing happens in a vacuum. Therefore, it's important for me to touch on both of these topics now. If you're philanthropic, then when you sell your company, you will likely put part of it in a Charitable Trust or Donor-Advised Fund. (Remember the story about Dr. VFO?) A Charitable Trust differs from a Donor-Advised Fund, but they function similarly.

Charitable Trust

Charitable Trusts allow you to eliminate the taxes on part of the sale of your business (or even 100 percent of your business—if you put the whole dollar amount in it. I don't necessarily recommend you do all of your business with Charitable Trusts, but you certainly can eliminate all the taxable gains by putting the business profits in a trust. Why not? Because it might not be in your best interest as it may not line up with your lifestyle plans. When you're talking about tax reduction, you can get rid of it all, but you have nothing left over for anything else.

If you're philanthropic, and you've got causes you want to support, then incorporate Elite Wealth Planning as you're doing your corporate Exit Planning. From there, you can tie those two pieces together from the very beginning, not the very end.

You can give the whole tree away and live off the fruit and never touch the tree again. This is what happens when you go 100 percent in with a Charitable Trust. Or you can live off the income from the trust, and then when you pass away, all the money goes to charity, but you've had an income stream for your entire lifetime.

It's like planting an apple tree. You can choose to cut down the apple tree, eat the apples, and burn the wood for warmth. Or you can prune the tree, eat some of the apples, and use some of the wood. Would you rather live and give from the root or the fruit?

Personal Wealth & Employee Stock Option Plans

It's critical for dental entrepreneurs to work on maximizing their personal wealth before the sale of the company because they go hand in hand. Don't simply do one and ignore the other. A great example of a well-planned and successful exit is with Dr. Exit. If your practice has twenty to forty million dollars of revenue with a substantial employee base like Dr. Exit, then you'll appreciate his story.

Employee Stock Ownership Plan Specialist

I was consulting a client, going down the employee stock ownership plan (ESOP). We were looking at selling the business to his employees. "Why would you recommend that?" you ask. First, the client didn't want to pay any taxes, so putting an ESOP in place eliminated most, if not all, of the capital gains on the sale of his business because he sold it to his employees instead of selling it to a corporate buyer (or another entity).

Doing so proved to be a huge success story because now he can give back to the people who helped him build his amazing company. Plus, they've got the ability to gain and grow wealth. As they continue to work hard in the company, they'll actually see the benefits from it because they're now shareholders. A board of directors will be appointed to run the company, but the owner can still be involved as little or as much as he wants. This example represents building a successful customized exit strategy. Typical ESOP transactions last about five to seven years, then the employees and the board of directors will run the company.

As the company continues to grow, my client can still get a second bite at the apple, so to speak, and participate in the growth of the company. Since his employees will share in the growth of the company, they will be rewarded for doing a good job.

There's a sweet spot for selling to an ESOP because if you do it too soon, you may not get the most value in terms of what you're looking for. Why? Because you are giving up that future growth. So you must decide: "At what point do I want to exit?" If you plan on exiting twelve years from now, then plan on six to eight months to set up an ESOP.

Wealth Transfer Updating Frequency

"How often should I be checking this?"

The answer to this question is not as much time-based as it is event-based. We call our companies Lifestone Companies because they center much of what we do around life events. If you start thinking event-based, then you're always going to be updated. If you think, *Hey, my daughter just had a new grandbaby. I'm going to go review my estate plan.* Excellent, you did it. If you acquire a new piece of property, you think, *Hey, is this in my trust? I should take a look at it.* Then make sure you do. That's why I would encourage you to think event-based, not time-based.

Estate Planning can help you transfer the wealth you've built according to your wishes, your desires, and your goals. When done correctly, you can get some tremendous tax benefits that allow more of the wealth to go where you want, instead of it going to the government.

Many business owners and dental entrepreneurs haven't taken advantage of all the things that are out there for them. This is why it's paramount to go back and take a second look.

Do you have advisors who are doing constant discovery with you and asking these questions? Discovery isn't a one-time meeting. It's a series of ongoing meetings where you're constantly refining your needs and wants.

I would tell you true Wealth Management in a true Virtual Family Office experience starts with discovery, continues with discovery, and ends with discovery. Your motto, like mine, should be: *"discovery, discovery, discovery!"* You should always have advisors who are truly interested in your business, your life goals, and who are constantly asking about *you.*

This is why you talk to someone like me! We can dive deeper and figure out when YOUR optimal timing is. Your goals and objectives should drive the timeline, not anything else.

Do You Have to Be a Dentist to Be in the Field of Dentistry?

Many dental entrepreneurs are trying to grow their practice and are looking for outside investors. One question remains: Do you have to be a dentist to own a dental practice? The answer? Yes, you do. Non-dentists cannot own a dental business. However, non-dentists can own a Dental Service Organization that provides services, goods, and support to dental practices that are owned by a dentist. There has been substantial growth in DSOs recently because they build a management structure and a support organization that supports practices.

What's a DSO?

A Dental Service Organization (DSO) is an organization that provides non-clinical services to dentists, helping their business to run smoother by providing advanced technologies (via state-of-the-art tools), facility maintenance, human resources, accounting, marketing, and continuing education to benefit the business and employees. The patients can benefit in many ways too: affordable healthcare, advanced technologies, and more time with the dentist—who isn't trying to also run the day-to-day operations and wearing himself thin!

Dr. VFO's Story of Wealth Transfer

Let me tell you about an impactful scenario I encountered with a family I had known for a while. It demonstrates how the Virtual Family Office really ties together leaving a legacy with transferring wealth.

One weekend, I was outside of Yosemite in a little town called Oakhurst with Dr. VFO. She had brought her brother, sister, and their spouses along. I helped Dr. VFO bring in a legacy planner. Unfortunately, her mother-in-law had just passed away. At this point, though, nothing happened with the trust. Their dad was still around, but you never know when someone's time will be up. He could be here for ten years, or just one year. Our goal was to prepare the family and get things ready for when he was not around.

From Dr. VFO's standpoint, she is her dad's only child. Her mom has three kids: her sister, brother, and herself (Dr. VFO). Their dad has one kid (Dr. VFO). So a total of three children were to inherit the estate. With their trust, the mom and dad split their estate in half because in California, all marital property is considered community property.

Dad said, *"I'm going to give all of my half to my daughter, Dr. VFO. She gets 50 percent."*

Mom comes along and says, *"Well, I'm going to divide my 50 percent evenly among my three kids."* Essentially, Dr. VFO gets two-thirds of the estate, and her brother and sister get a sixth of the estate. When you're talking about close to $10 million, that's a pretty big difference.

We wanted to bring in a legacy planner and to start explaining these things because avoiding litigation is vitally important. This scenario could easily turn into a long protracted fight over assets, questioning why the mom and dad did things the way they did.

So they brought in a legacy planner and started working through these decisions.

All of this required four months of preparation while working with Cindy Arledge, a member of my family office, who also just happens to be one of the leaders in legacy planning.

Through this process, it was beautiful to watch the siblings come together and hash through issues and share things they've never shared before.

Being that I had known Dr. VFO and her family for many years, I saw the impact in real time that this process had on her family and how it created positive conversations and interactions between the family members, who eventually opened up discussions of life topics that mattered to each of them.

During this process, I wanted them to consider this question: What does legacy mean?

Sure, they're going to get some money, but what does *legacy* actually look like for each of them?

Watching the family come together was powerful. Having the legacy planner there to work through this process of the financial data and the details of life that will follow this plan was immeasurable.

- What are the emotions?
- What's important to you?

- What do you want to have happen?
- How do you work within the rules of the trust to help you achieve your goals?

Dr. VFO is a trustee. This whole process affected not just her immediate family and herself, but her own family as well. They were already looking at ways they could accelerate some of the payouts or buy out her brother and sister early. Her sister was in her sixties, while her husband was seventy-five years old. Once again, not a lot of runway left. If the dad lasted another ten years, he would be eighty-five. The money wouldn't do a whole lot of good then. So we wondered if there were ways to accelerate this and help give them funds earlier or buy them outright? How could we best support them in that moment?

Part of the meeting was coming together as a family and discussing these things and finding out what was important to everyone.

- How can we discuss options in a peaceful way?
- How can we decide on a plan that addresses all the needs of the beneficiaries and the owner of the trust?

That's all part of the Wealth Transfer.

Wrapping up Wealth Transfer

So often, we think Wealth Transfer is simply about passing on money to the next generation. The reality is that wealth can create a lot of problems, just like the story above. What better way to pass wealth down and create a legacy than by leaving money to the next generation? Imagine doing that and avoiding the family feuds, giving to the people who matter, all while becoming better people in the process?

That's the true definition and intent of Wealth Transfer: the ability to bring your family together and have hard conversations while everyone walks away stronger because there's a well-thought-out plan in place.

But with wealth comes people who want to take it...

This brings us to the third element of Advanced Planning: Wealth Protection. This involves protecting everything you've worked so hard for from being unjustly taken.

Wealth Protection

Chapter 4

"Beware of those who want to benefit from your hard work."

We live in a litigious society. In my experience, the largest targets of lawsuits are neither the people worth a few million dollars nor the people worth hundreds of millions! Instead, those most likely to be involved in lawsuits are situated right in the middle with a net worth of about five to fifty million dollars—the small business owners or middle-class millionaires, such as yourself.

Chances are, you don't have an attorney on retainer who works just for you. So if you get subjected to litigation, you're going to panic—and rightfully so. Sometimes it's easier to pay the bozo off and move on with your life. You simply want to settle and make your legal nightmare go away as quickly as possible so you can get back to life.

This is completely understandable. As a business owner, you've worked very hard to achieve a certain level of success. Unfortunately, there are people out there who want to benefit from your success without having done any of the hard work.

The question you must ask is: "How can I protect my money from being unjustly taken via lawsuits, divorce, or natural disasters—such as floods, forest fires, and earthquakes?"

The answer? Wealth Protection.

Another question to ask is: "What is the role of insurance in asset protection?"

This chapter will walk you through the preparation process of protecting your wealth, resulting in 1) maintaining confidence during an unforeseen crisis, and 2) safeguarding your money so you keep more in the bank. Remember, it's not how much you *make*; it's how much you *keep*. It is possible to face litigious circumstances and come out with barely a scratch, financially speaking.

You've always got the government coming for a portion of your wealth via taxes, but there are others who will try to come after your money and threaten your wealth, such as someone slipping or falling at your business. The time to plan a winning strategy is before things happen. First, let's cover some insurance basics:

- Do you have the proper amount of insurance coverage for any lawsuit you might face?

- Have you reviewed your current policies?

- Do you know how your policies all fit together? Could they be better tailored to fit your needs?

- How well are you protected against lawsuits and litigation? It's possible you are an open target and don't even know it.

According to the National Federation of Independent Business, small business owners pay an estimated $35 billion each year out-of-pocket to settle unjust claims or divorce fees. Instead of waiting for a crisis to happen, it's imperative to be proactive and come up with ways to protect yourself and your business.

What strategies and tactics have *you* put in place recently to protect yourself?

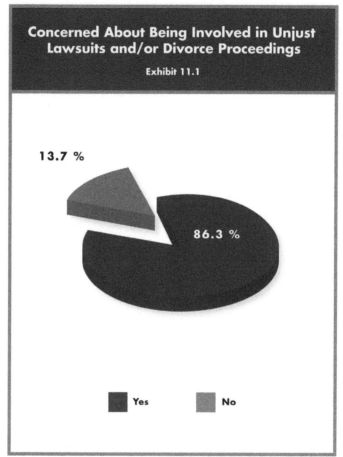

Concerned About Being Involved in Unjust Lawsuits and/or Divorce Proceedings

Exhibit 11.1

13.7 %

86.3 %

■ Yes ■ No

N = 262 Successful Business Owners. Source: AES Nation.

Looking at the data, 86.3% of business owners are absolutely concerned about being involved in some kind of unjust lawsuit or divorce proceedings. While it's almost impossible to avoid certain situations, there are strategies and plans that you can put in place to protect you when something unfortunate *does* happen.

Premarital Planning Asset Protection Discussion

When most people hear the term prenuptial agreement (also known as a premarital agreement), they assume it's because one of the parties does not trust the other. True, in many instances that is the case. But there is also a very savvy reason couples who fully trust one another choose to have a premarital agreement, and it's all related to *preserving and protecting their money as a couple* if either of them gets sued by someone outside the marriage. A premarital agreement is one way (among many) to safeguard your assets legally so they are a little bit harder to get to.

Once you overcome the common misconception that you only use premarital agreements if something goes bad in the relationship down the road, you will be eager to take advantage of this wealth protection tip. The following real-life example provides a good reason for you and your spouse (or future spouse) to place this business strategy into the mix. But a premarital agreement is not just for divorce; it also protects a couple's assets.

Premarital Case Study

A few years ago, litigation took place with Dr. Middle of Your Career. He was married to a woman who was also a business owner, and they had a premarital agreement in place. They kept all their assets separate. Unfortunately, the husband ended up getting sued. He went down a long legal journey and finally ended up in mediation.

He recalled the day as if it were yesterday. The mediators started pacing in and out of the room. And one of them finally came back and sat down with the husband and said, *"Well, you're not willing to give us enough money. The other guy is looking to settle for a lot more. Your wife owns both a house and a business, correct?"*

The husband looked at his attorney and asked, *"Is now the right time to tell him?"*

The attorney nodded his head and replied, *"Yeah, now's a great time to tell him."*

The husband looked back at the mediator and said, *"My wife and I have a premarital arrangement. My wife's assets belong only to her."*

Imagine the look of fear and disappointment that appeared on the mediator's face. You could see he wasn't going to get what he wanted. *"I'll be right back,"* he said, then came back a short while later with a number that was significantly lower than what they had originally asked for.

What Dr. Middle of Your Career had was a premarital agreement— *or prenup.*

This is a couple who was, and still is, happily married. When they decided to get married, they said to each other, *"Hey, we're both business owners. We actually face the risk of litigation someday. Let's put security measures in place, not because we're planning for divorce, but because we want to protect each other."*

The prenup allowed them to keep all their property separate. Anything they acquired during the marriage was not jointly owned. There was zero community property created in the relationship, which resulted in a reduced combined loss in the case of a lawsuit.

That one strategic move saved them over half a million dollars in settlements and legal fees. Not to mention the ongoing headaches, nightmares, and stress of pending litigation without a guaranteed outcome. It sent the other side away, saying, *"Oh, we can't get to the wife's assets because they're hers. They don't belong to the husband."*

You may be wondering how the mediators were unaware of their premarital agreement. When the plaintiff's attorney was doing discovery, they never did *proper* discovery. All he knew was that the wife owned a house and dental practice. But he failed to ask if there was a premarital agreement in place. Had he known, he never would have never pushed for the large settlement. Because their legal team failed to do discovery, it ended up costing the plaintiff a lot of time and effort instead of presenting the defendant a lower figure up front.

That's what wealth protection does; it protects your assets. It forces the other side to back down because they realize they don't have access to certain sources of money (and assets) they thought they did.

Umbrella Insurance

According to John Bowen and Russ Allen Prince, two people I'm pleased to call my friends, they stress the importance of personal umbrella policies. These policies are often overlooked and under-used, even by the affluent. It is, however, a significant component of a rock-solid Wealth Protection plan.

Having an umbrella policy in place can protect you from many scenarios that could lead to lawsuits. Do you have significant assets to protect? If your answer is yes, then let's look at the benefits of having an umbrella policy in place.

The biggest and most common assets we think about when we hear the word *insurance* is your car and your home. You have insurance policies set in place for those, but do you have enough coverage for your personal wealth?

According to Elite Wealth Management, "Most insurance policies top out at around $500,000 of liability coverage." If, God forbid, you find yourself in a situation where someone gets hurt or seriously injured on your property, they are likely to seek more than your $500,000 cap. What do you do in that circumstance? This is where the umbrella policy shines. It could cover the balance that remains when your liability insurance tops out, allowing you to keep your personal assets.

Here are some questions to ask yourself when assessing your insurance coverage:

- Do you have enough coverage? How much is it?
- How do you determine if your umbrella policy covers the gap where your other insurance ends? "A general rule of thumb is that if your net worth is $20 million or less, make sure your umbrella policy covers what you're worth. If you are worth more than $20 million, it becomes a question of how much risk you're comfortable taking on." *(Elite Wealth Management, pg. 2)*

A smart move by many Ultra-Wealthy dental entrepreneurs is getting as large and as comprehensive of an umbrella policy as possible. The odds are in *your* favor, and it's unlikely that you'll reach the limit of the policy or the possible financial downside from a serious accident and substantial lawsuit. *(Elite Wealth Management pg. 3)*.

The great thing is that an umbrella policy is generally inexpensive to purchase. Plus, it's a quick win. In less than half an hour you can have a conversation with your insurance agent and discuss the best ranges that work for you.

Very few business owners have any kind of wealth protection plan in place for their assets. In fact, research suggests that only 27.5 percent do. This is a massive missed opportunity for you as a dental entrepreneur to protect yourself. I hope this encourages you to consider further protecting yourself personally and protecting your business.

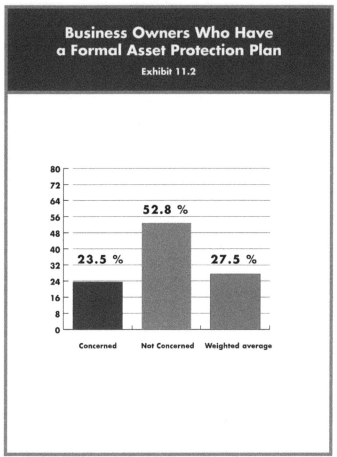

N = 262 Successful Business Owners. Source: AES Nation.

Five Ways to Protect Your Assets

1. Get protected before a claim is made against you.

This could be self-explanatory, but many business professionals fail to plan ahead for the what-if scenarios. However, making this move could cost you. As with any insurance plan, the best time to have it is *before* you need it. Therefore, start including your asset protection during your business planning phase!

2. Cover the basics.

Evaluating your liability insurance and other policies will secure your foundation.

3. **Consider a variety of other asset protection strategies.**

There are many strategic options you could have, depending on your specific situation. Therefore review *all* your choices, including but not limited to property-casualty insurance, such as auto, rental, and personal excess; liability insurance; health insurance; and disability insurance. Other considerations to be aware of are state law insurance exemptions and various forms of ownership. Discuss these coverages with your professional to find the best protection strategies for you.

4. **Be sure your attorney or other professionals are qualified to help you protect your assets.**

As we'll briefly touch on, you'll find that there are many professionals out there who aren't necessarily in a position to provide the best guidance for your asset protection planning. It's important that you assess where mistakes can be made before committing. Learn more in number five (and in Chapter 7).

5. **Avoid big mistakes that will trip up your asset protection efforts.**

It could be a challenge to gain all the details and understanding of how the protection strategies work in order for them to be executed effectively. If not structured appropriately, the strategies may not hold water when they are needed most. It's so easy to overlook things and to simply make mistakes.

The Biggest Asset-Protection Planning Mistakes and How to Avoid Them.

Starting your asset protection planning *after* you are aware you can be sued

The last thing you want is to run into a claim where you find yourself scrambling to move your assets around. Your intent may be good, but it's impossible to know what someone was thinking. This could be considered a fraudulent conveyance. Courts will look at "badges of fraud," which is circumstantial evidence of actual fraud. Unfortunately, your action of moving your assets in response to a claim you weren't prepared for will trigger this, placing you in the crosshairs of the courts. The best way to avoid this is to set your asset protection planning in place as early as possible. *(EWG, Five Big Asset Protection Planning Mistakes-and How to Avoid Them, pg 2).*

Not having enough (or the proper) liability insurance

Many business owners do not have the right kinds or amounts of liability insurance to meet their needs. Of course, while you can't predict the future, you can stress test your liability coverage. Doing this could help you discover and correct any gaps found in your coverage.

Failing to approach asset-protection planning synergistically with your other Elite Wealth Planning efforts

It's important to consider all the components of your financial life, including estate planning, income-tax planning, and asset-protection planning. Think of asset planning like a puzzle piece in your holistic approach to Elite Wealth Planning. Taking this approach will help you understand things from the bigger picture allowing you to weigh the trade-offs and the risks.

Not understanding what you did and why you did it

You're a strategically minded person who runs a successful business. Your brain and, of course, your individual talents got you here. Many of your big-business decisions were done with planning and research on the front end, right? Though asset protection can become quite complicated, you don't need to be an expert in the specific strategies. However, when you plan your asset protection, feel confident about expressing your intended results, and be able to explain why you did what you did.

Failing to work with a skilled professional

Lastly, though *very* important, you want to work with the best professional for you. This seems obvious, but there are many Pretenders and Predators out there who claim expertise. In reality, though, they could do more harm than good. Stay tuned for Chapter 7 when we dive more into these so-called *"experts."* For now, be aware that in order for you to get the optimal benefits of the asset protection you are seeking, you need to work with someone who is recognized by other financial professionals as an expert on asset protection planning.

Captive Insurance Companies

While you're considering various types of protection, another great coverage to know about is called captive insurance. Captive Insurance companies allow you to design the property and casualty coverage unique to your business. With this coverage, you'll gain greater control over your tax liability. You can even wrap certain things into this insurance company that may not be covered by traditional policies.

How Is Captive Insurance Used?

Usually, traditional policies are streamlined into one core structure. With Captive Insurance, however, there is an option called a "cell captive." Many larger businesses have taken advantage of traditional Captive Insurance policies, and it's easy to see why. The benefits are great, such as better risk management, favorable tax treatment, and lower insurance costs. However, Captive Insurance companies have one challenge: the expense involved for the insurer in setup costs and maintenance.

That's where cell captives come into play.

For many small and mid-size businesses, cell captives could be a great option. It is a low-cost way to get involved in the Captive Insurance arena while still benefiting.

Many of these benefits include:

- Lower setup costs
- Lower initial capital and surplus
- A stepping-stone to a single-parent insurance company

However, there are some disadvantages, too, to be aware of.

- Distributions are taxed as long-term dividends.
- Liquidation of the cell is taken as long-term capital gains.
- The underwriting profit is tax-deferred, but you are taxed annually.

These are the options you have to weigh out, and to help you, you can visit: *Www.DentalWealthNationBook.com* to download a full report on Captive Insurance Companies.

Ultimately, Captive Insurance allows you to "underwrite at your own risk." As the business owner, you now get far more control. You can wrap things into a captive, like a brand reputation risk.

You may have heard the unfortunate story about a dentist who went on a safari, only to come back with his practice in ruins. Walter Palmer went safari hunting and shot a lion. Of course, it ended up all over

Facebook and social media. That didn't bode so well for his business. His whole practice got boycotted and essentially shut down.

Now, I'm not recommending you set up a Captive Insurance policy so you can go lion hunting, but something stupid will happen one day that could put your brand at risk that is best covered under a Captive Insurance policy, doing this can help protect your business.

If that dentist had a Captive Insurance company, he would have been able to pull large sums out of their insurance company for that specific risk enabling him to handle the business interruption somewhat seamlessly—by hiring a PR firm.

I'm not suggesting you should go set up Captive Insurance so you can do bad things intentionally; however, everything is subjective nowadays. Unfortunately, it's no longer a matter of *if* but *when*. For instance, you may put the "wrong" thing on Twitter—or any social media for that matter. These days, we don't have to guess what it can do to someone's career. Or what it can do to *your career, your business* that you've worked so hard for.

Think about the liability for Jurassic Park, a theme park in the fictional movie where dinosaurs are being recreated and reborn in today's world. This park is a perfect example. The owners should have a Captive Insurance company in case the dinosaurs were to get loose and start eating everyone. There certainly is a real risk. But the theme park owners won't find an insurance carrier on the face of the planet who's willing to write a policy for that possibility. If you have your own Captive Insurance company, though, you can certainly have coverage for this (possible) catastrophic event.

While the story of Jurassic Park is fictional, there's nothing fictional about:

- Big-game hunting
- Deep-sea fishing
- Sharing a family photo at a Memorial Day Parade with the "wrong" candidate's flag in the background
- Attending the "wrong" church
- Driving an electric vehicle, or a gas car—or both!

These are just a few scenarios of what a Captive Insurance plan can help protect against.

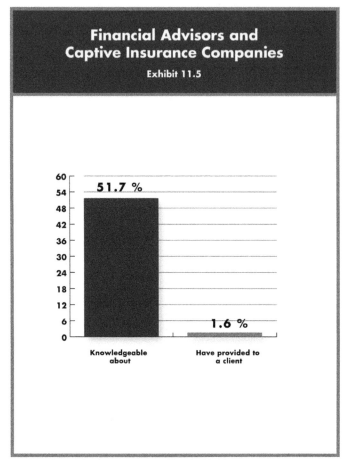

N = 803 Financial Advisors. Source: CEG Worldwide.

In a study of 803 financial advisors, 51 percent are knowledgeable in the area of Captive Insurance. However, only 1.6 percent have implemented a Captive Insurance company for one client. This is an incredible missed opportunity.

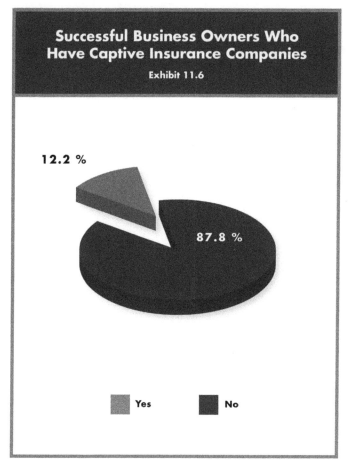

Successful Business Owners Who Have Captive Insurance Companies

Exhibit 11.6

12.2 %

87.8 %

Yes   No

N = 262 Successful Business Owners. Source: AES Nation.

Out of 262 successful business owners surveyed, 87 percent do not have Captive Insurance companies in place for their business. Most people, possibly even yourself, have traditional insurance. You could be buying from a captive local agent who works for a well-known insurance company, such as State Farm, who is only able to sell that insurance company's product.

As you move up the scale, you'll determine it's more efficient to work with an insurance broker. An insurance broker is not captive to one specific insurance company. They can go out to the marketplace and shop the policy among different insurance companies. Oftentimes, they can get you better rates, resulting in lower premiums and an increase in coverage.

Captive Insurance is the equivalent of having your own insurance company with you as the business owner. You have ownership, which means you actually own the insurance company. Establishing Captive Insurance typically takes some time and planning, but it's not too arduous. You can get it up and running in about a month to a month and a half. Essentially, by setting up a Captive Insurance company, you write a check to your own insurance company, but the funds are yours, and you get to manage them.

Before you start exploring your options, I urge you to do an analysis of your existing policies and decide what you want to cover. Be careful using captives though. If you misuse them, you will get in trouble. If you set one up without a legitimate purpose, the IRS will come for you. If you use them correctly, you will be happy to have them when and if the day comes to activate the benefits. For example, would you buy title wave insurance coverage if your practice is in the middle of Ohio? That certainly makes little sense, but allow me to give you an example of what *does* work. As we explained earlier, cell captives could be very beneficial to business owners if the cost of traditional insurance is much higher. There are ways in which some entrepreneurs are using cell captives.

Case Study 1

You may have heard of Acme Dental Corp. They employ 268 employees. Through one calendar year, up to April 2017, they paid $2.7 million in medical insurance for their employees. Around that time, it was to be renewed with a premium of $3.2 million. At this point, Acme Dental Corp considered a cell captive could be a great option for all their employees. In just a twelve-month period, by April 2018, the firm's total medical spending reduced to $2.2 million! Not only that, but they had a total maximum cost of $1.9 million. The cell captive they created saved them over $1 million. Can you fight with that?

Case Study 2

With many hidden gems, so many business owners do not take advantage of Captive Insurance. Out of 262, only 12.2 percent actually have! Let's break down an example of how much having a captive in place could impact a business.

"Through their ownership of a captive insurance company, the business owners projected in five years' time to be approximately $4.7

million ahead of where they would be should they elect to continue using only traditional insurance to cover their risks." *(Becoming Seriously Wealthy, Ex11.6 pg 107)*

As we covered earlier, you may be worried about being sued, but you may not have taken any action to put safeguards in place. It's imperative to examine how to control the risks of a business, via employment agreements, buy-sells, as well as other vehicles to assist in protecting your wealth.

How do you structure your assets and legal ownership—whether it's trust or limited liability entities—to put your wealth beyond the reach of creditors or other people who want to take it?

First, remember there are rules and regulations you have to comply with. It's an eight-inch line, and you want to be careful you don't step right over it. Next, determine how you will build your plan for Wealth Protection: You can go the route of Dr. DIY, taking your own time to learn all the ins and outs of regulations and compliance. Or, if you prefer, you can reach out to me, like Dr. VFO did, and take some of the pressure off yourself. I'd be happy to assist.

This is what my team and I will do for you—take the pressure and weight off so you can focus on running your day-to-day business with your patients. The analysis costs nothing. We'll sit down and figure out the specific coverages you need and which ones you don't. We then work toward a target premium of what you'd like to pay and what risk you'd like to cover.

This all ties right back into discovery.

- Maybe this is right for you.

- Maybe you only require a good umbrella policy.

- Maybe you only need to do an insurance audit and make sure everything's covered.

- If you really want to take it to the next level, then do a captive. Maybe it fits your goals; maybe it doesn't.

Either way, do discovery.

Remember, with Wealth Transfer, it's about taking care of your heirs. You want to facilitate that process in the most tax-efficient way, and pass those assets on to the people you love, and you want to do so in a way with minimal difficulty and cost, in order to make sure your heirs will benefit to the fullest extent possible.

With Wealth Protection, it's about protecting your wealth against catastrophic loss, potential creditors, litigation, children, spouses, potential ex-spouses, and identity theft, ensuring that your assets are not unjustly taken.

Dr. Middle of Career (MOC)

We've been talking about the Wealth Management Formula. Now we're on the third element of Advanced Planning called Wealth Protection. As a reminder, the Wealth Management Formula states that Wealth Management is equal to investment consulting—plus advanced planning, plus relationship management.

The beauty of Wealth Management is that none of these things happen in isolation. While a Captive Insurance company helps you protect your assets against being unjustly taken and helps with the insurance side of things, it can also help with Wealth Enhancement.

Dr. MOC (Middle of Your Career) is a very successful dentist and runs several practices. I helped him set up a captive insurance company several years ago. We put the dental warranty program in place. We put in officers and directors, and liability insurance was also in place. Plus, we established employment practices liabilities. He has been able to get very substantial write-offs—close to one $1.2 million in his captive in just three years!

Dr. MOC also decided that he wanted to sell off his practice. He was fifty years old, very successful, and had reached a point where he was tired of carrying the weight of ownership. The weight of ownership feels heavy when you're the only one carrying the practice.

After looking into fourteen different buyers, he finally found a group that was going to buy his practice. It took about a year for the transaction to go through, so the process required patience. When you sell your practice, there are certain risks associated with doing so. You offer certain warranties and representations to the new buyers about your financials. There may be financial targets you are required to hit in order to receive the full payout from the sale of your practice. Selling your practice is risky business, but don't forget there's a Wealth Protection component.

When you sell your practice, like Dr. VFO did in an earlier story, and like Dr. MOC selling his practice here, you're going to have one of those Lifestone moments. Why? Because in selling your business, you'll receive the highest income (or biggest payday) of your entire life—likely occurring in a single year.

Your Wealth Protection success comes back to how well we've protected your assets. The first concern is how to mitigate some of your taxes. Well, in the case of Dr. MOC, because there was risk in the transaction, I called up the captive manager, Wes, and said, "Hey, Wes, we're doing this transaction. Can we allocate some funds to the insurance company for the risk of this transaction in case something happens?" Because Dr. MOC had a Captive Insurance company set up, he could put an additional $1 million in his captive pre-tax to help mitigate the risk of this $22 million transaction. Out of that $8 million of capital that he was set to receive up front, he could put a million dollars of that into a captive pre-tax. That saved him over half a million dollars in taxes in one move.

How quickly can we do these things? In one afternoon! In one conversation, actually, because we've been following this Wealth Management framework and looking at these things holistically, not in isolation. In one conversation, we could save Dr. MOC half a million dollars in taxes.

That's the power of Wealth Protection, powered by discovery and viewed holistically within the Wealth Management Formula.

You may have an advisor who only focuses on Asset Protection or Wealth Protection, but they're missing the bigger picture. You may have a CPA who only focuses on tax planning, but they're missing the bigger picture too.

That's the power of a Virtual Family Office, having a team who coordinates all the moving puzzle pieces for you.

This brings us to the fourth and final element of Advanced Planning, which is how you can make an even bigger impact on the causes that matter most to you—Charitable Gifting and making an impact through meaningful gifts.

Charitable Gifting

Chapter 5

"Giving your money away will bring you great joy."

Many times, people think giving is just about money, but it's not. Giving also requires your time, talents, abilities—and finding out what you're good at. There are so many avenues of giving, including donating to a cause, helping a family, investing in someone's education, volunteering in the community, sharing your knowledge and skills for free—the list is endless.

In addition to Wealth Enhancement, Wealth Protection, and Wealth Transfer, the fourth primary concern of many dental entrepreneurs is Charitable Gifting.

Having a heart for giving really comes down to what Scripture says: "One who is faithful in a very little is also faithful in much, and one who is dishonest in a very little is also dishonest in much" Luke 16:10 (ESV).

Approximately one-third of people are considered charitable but lack a well-thought-out plan to maximize the impact of their money once it's channeled into philanthropic means. They also lack clear guidance on instilling values to the people they love, who will also be good candidates for future giving.

One of the most important parts of Charitable Gifting is *how* you give money. Your values and interests will drive *who* gets your money, so you want that organization, person, or group to benefit from your strategic planning, leaving no money wasted, no investment dollars sitting in the wrong places—and less going to the IRS. This way, you can magnify what you're doing and impact your recipients more deeply. Sounds pretty good, right? So why is so much charitable money untapped?

Unfortunately, according to CEG Worldwide, only 6.8 percent of financial advisors and wealth managers proactively offer or do any form of advanced planning. The irony is that this is the stage where you get the most value from your hard-earned money.

For example, if I get you an extra .5 or 1 percent on your investment portfolio, it's going to have minimal impact. Let's say you have a 10 million portfolio. If you receive an additional 1 percent return, that's an extra $100,000 you've earned that year. If you decide to sell your company and we do proper tax planning—sheltering a large portion of it from taxes—we may save you two or three million dollars. That strategy provides a much higher yield and has a further impact than an extra 1 percent return on your portfolio.

Impact Discussion

The impact and the legacy you want to leave is our next focus. If you stop and think about your future, both from a business and personal standpoint, what is it that's driving you to achieve your goals?

Maybe you want to continue to care for the people who matter to you, the people you love, your immediate family members, your extended family, your employees, and possibly a close friend. Taking care of everyone in your circle is what drives you to work hard and leave the world a better place because you were here.

It's not only the driven dentists who are interested in supporting important causes. Warren Buffett, one of the world's richest men, has pledged to give away 99 percent of his wealth. In fact, Bill Gates, founder of Microsoft, as well as many other billionaires, have joined forces, committing to give away over half of their fortune. You can learn more and see who the pledges are at: www.GivingPledge.org.

You most likely don't have billions of dollars to give away. However, if you're like many of my incredible clients, you do want to make an impact on the world with your wealth. Doing so could be as simple as what Dr. Exit did for one of his employees: "Mrs. Value" was the acting controller for Dr. Exit and a valued employee. Her life expenses increased due to unforeseen medical issues. Dr. Exit said, "Hey if you need ten grand, I'd be happy to make a gift to you. I can wire it to your account. I care about you and want you to be okay."

Dr. Exit had a caring heart, business savvy, and the knowledge to help her without actually losing ten thousand dollars based on *how* he gave her the money. Keep reading on the ways you can give . . . so everyone benefits!

The Charitable Planning Process

When it comes to charitable planning, clients can easily become overwhelmed by their options and unsure of how to start. Like most things in life, if you establish a process and see successful ways others have channeled their money, it becomes much easier. Similar to the Wealth Management Formula, Charitable Gifting provides a framework that maximizes your financial impact and provides clarity that your money will be directed to the proper channels and appropriately managed. It's important to understand all the benefits you and your family will receive as a result of steering your wealth outward into the community with a solid plan in place.

The first benefit involves your family. Instilling philanthropic values in the people you love is so important, providing you the opportunity to include the next generation in your humanitarian pursuits.

The second benefit of having a Charitable Gifting plan helps you focus and streamline your giving by asking yourself key questions: How much do I want to give? When do I want to begin giving? What is my budget for giving? What requests for giving are not in line with my goals? How can I say no when someone requests a donation that's outside of my plan?

The third major benefit of having a Charitable Gifting planning process is maximizing your wealth by enhancing and maximizing your tax benefits. This circles back to the entire Wealth Management Formula. The biggest impact of your giving will significantly affect your bottom line on taxes.

The fourth benefit of having a Charitable Gifting planning process is that it allows you to fully support your values. The more carefully you think through what's important to you, and the different vehicles for giving that are available to you, the more likely the giving is going to support the things that you value.

As an entrepreneur, your foundation thrives on structure and process, right? Now that you are excited about the benefits of the process, let's look at the steps for making a Charitable Gifting plan.

- Step One: Formulate your goals.

- Step Two: Decide *where* to give.

- Step Three: Decide *when* to give.

- Step Four: Decide *what* to give.

When it comes to that planning process, I want to recognize my mentors, John Bowen and Russ Allen Prince, and credit them for creating the cutting-edge work they've done with mapping out the charitable gifting process.

STEP ONE: Formulate your goals.

This step is multifaceted. When you give, you want to make sure that you're giving to organizations and pursuits that advance your deepest values. Some of the questions you can ask as you're formulating your goals are:

- What matters most to you?

- What makes you laugh?

- What makes you cry?

- What grabs your emotions?

If you've ever watched a YouTube video about animals being rescued, does that touch your heart? Does it trigger a desire in you to help animals? Or is that of no interest to you? That's someone else's jam. Or have you watched videos about orphans, widows, or people who are building water wells in Africa? What do you actually care about most? What fascinates you? What challenges you to always learn more? What causes out there prompt you to take action and get involved?

Examining what you care about helps you formulate your goal.

Next, what values do you actually want to convey with your giving?

- Do you want to give back to the community?

- Do you want to promote something?

- Do you want to help sustain your church or support arts and culture?

Now think about what you want to *achieve* with your Charitable Gifting. How do you want the person, cause, or organization to look once they benefit from your gifts? Define exactly what you want to impact. Is it a geographical focus? Is it international? Is it something local in your community? Is it nationwide?

How do you want to be involved? Do you simply want to give gifts and let the organization run with it? Or do you want to be deeply involved in the choices that are being made?

In summary, Step One helps you dig deep to formulate your goals.

- What do you *care* about most?
- What *values* do you want to convey with your giving?
- What do you hope to *achieve* with your giving?
- Where do you want to make an *impact?*
- How do you want to be *involved* in the giving?

STEP TWO: Decide where to give.

This may sound simple, but *how* you want to give plays off of *where* you end up giving.

- Do you want to deepen a relationship with an existing charity?
- Do you want to start your own organization?
- How do you want to give as you begin that search?

Explore and talk to some of the charities you've been supporting. Ask around your community, then branch out further if you see a need in another country. Remember: make sure that *where* you give aligns with your goals.

STEP THREE: Decide *when* to give.

The timing of your gifts matter, as we've talked about in the previous chapters. Tying in a Charitable Gifting strategy also helps with annual gifting. If you're selling your business and you know you've got the highest taxable income of your career, then why not pre-fund the giving for the rest of your life and get a big charitable deduction, which will help reduce your income in that moment of when you have the most income? That's the year to pre-fund the giving for the rest of your life.

Timing matters. You want to be strategic in planning *when* to give.

- Do you want to set up annual gifting?

- Do you want to prepare a legacy gifting?

- Do you want to give in response to a crisis?

- Do you want to give in response to a major financial windfall that's occurred?

Depending on what's going on in your life, you may end up with several of those strategies, one of those strategies, or something else. You can also decide on monthly, annual, or quarterly giving.

STEP FOUR: Decide what to give.

As you look at your assets, you'll figure out there are different ways that you can give. Cash is always one way to define *what* to give. No one's going to say no to that offering.

If you get creative, you can look into giving appreciated stock. We talked about some of those examples in other chapters. By giving stock, you will not be subject to the capital gains tax. Tangible property is another example of *what* to give. You can give clothing, autos, real estate, or even a portion of your business. Gifting tangible property allows you tax deductions. There are certain limitations, though, so have your advisor be thorough in helping you make the best Wealth Management Plan. You can also give your time and expertise to an organization through volunteering.

Donor-Advised Funds

A great way to leave your impact and legacy is with a Donor-Advised Fund, which is typically established by a financial services firm who manages the day-to-day operations. You, as the donor, make irrevocable contributions to the fund, and those assets are invested to grow tax-free. You can then recommend which charities should receive a gift, and the Donor-Advised Fund makes the grants on your behalf.

Sure, you can certainly endure all the work and set up your own private foundation with a board of directors. At some point, that may make sense for you, especially as you transition out of your full-time career. If you start your own foundation, you can continue to have some tax write-offs, so that's one large benefit. By establishing a Donor-Advised Fund, you can set up your own private foundation without having the administrative fees and the reporting requirements that come with a foundation.

You want to know what matters, so let's conduct an experiment. Take a minute and grab your phone or tablet. Look at your bank account and your calendar, then ask yourself:

- Where is my money going?
- What do I value?
- What do I care about the most?

Your bank account and calendar will be the most honest and transparent way to show you what you care about the most because where you go, who you spend your time with, and what you spend your money on is where your treasures are stored.

You may discover that the way you spend your time, money, and talents does not align with what's really important to you, revealing that your life is actually in a state of dissonance. You may find that you're not spending your time and money in a way that harmonizes with your value system.

By identifying your values and remaining true to them, an example is set for your family to also live through their value system. Your heart is part of your legacy, not just your money. By giving money to your family and to the people who matter, you model a high level of character. So when you say to your kids, "Hey, there's actually something more important than money—*having an impact* with that money," they understand both the cycle of wealth and legacy.

It's simple. You can set up a Donor-Advised Fund and then, throughout the year, have conversations with your kids and with your spouse: "Hey, we've got this pile of money that's set aside for giving. That's what it's for."

- "Who would you like to give money to?"
- "Why does giving this money to a specific person, cause, or organization matter to you?"
- "Tell me about what you value."

It's a great way to start some amazing conversations with your kids and other people in your circle who matter. You can deepen the conversation by asking, "How do you want to have an impact? Because I've set aside money for you to support things you're passionate about."

How Is Money Set Up in a Donor-Advised Fund?

With a Donor-Advised Fund, you can contribute with a recurring investment or even in a lump sum—or both ways, tailored to your wants and needs. Some will have a fantastic year and decide, "I've taken plenty of business tax deductions, and I'd like some additional write-offs. Let's contribute $100,000 to my Donor-Advised Fund."

It sounds like an exciting tool to have, doesn't it?

Few dental entrepreneurs know about this great tool. Unfortunately, the advisors they work with just don't inform them about it, and that's not your fault. You rely on individuals. You rely on financial professionals to help you know what you don't know. The numbers you know, as a dentist, are one to thirty-two. Those are your numbers, and you rely on your team. Chances are, your team isn't bringing you these ideas, because we know that less than one in ten financial advisors has ever done this for one client. What a huge missed opportunity for you.

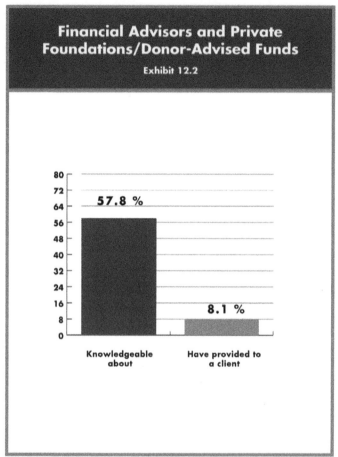

Financial Advisors and Private Foundations/Donor-Advised Funds

Exhibit 12.2

N = 803 Financial Advisors, Source: CEG Worldwide.

I am here to encourage and show you that having the right tools can dramatically enhance and transform your personal and business life. We want to make sure you have the knowledge to empower your decisions, to move you where you've always wanted to go, but didn't know how to get there.

Think back to when you looked at your bank account in the exercise I gave you earlier. Of course, you have priorities. You have bills to pay. You need to feed yourself and your family, and life seems to get busier every day. You've always felt charitably inclined. It's nagged at you, and you've been wanting to leave an impact and help others, but your everyday routine keeps taking precedence by default.

Now imagine waking up tomorrow and going about your everyday routine and checking your bank account again. This time, you feel elated to see that you *are* investing in the charities you care about, and you didn't even have to think about it. You didn't have to change your day. The Donor-Advised Fund, which only took you a small portion of your time, is moving all the pieces for you. It has jump-started a new charitable present and future for you and the ones you love. The best part is that you only need to sit back and watch in joy.

Look, I can feel your excitement jumping through the pages! You want to do this, but you're thinking, *How do I move it up the priority list?*

I encourage you to not equate prioritizing Charitable Gifting with cleaning your dining room table. ("*Oh, I'll get to it.*") There are so many benefits to doing it now. It's important, and you can't get the time back. Why wait to start leaving your legacy's lasting impact?

At this point in your career, I don't think you're waking up solely thinking, *How can I make more money today?* You're most likely thinking, *How can I make more money today and have the greatest impact on the world around me?*

You're focused on: *How can I decrease taxes, increase my impact, and leave my lasting legacy.*

The same was true for Dr. Exit, who is an amalgam of several clients blended together to help illustrate concepts for you. If you recall, he was getting ready to list his multiple dental practices for sale. His total valuation was close to twenty-seven million.

We started to engage in Pre-Sale Planning, and through the **Dental Wealth Nation Unlimited Discovery Process**™, we talked about his charitable intent. We also tied this into how to reduce his capital gain taxes when he sells. He looked at almost half of the $27 million dollars going to taxes. He also decided to involve his two daughters in his Charitable Gifting.

Dr. Exit chose to transfer $1,000,000 of his dental practice shares to a charitable trust, which would then sell the shares—and *not* be subject to taxes. Dr. Exit would receive a tax deduction of $1,000,000.

The money in the charitable trust would not be taxed until distribution. The funds inside of the charitable trust would also receive greater growth than funds outside of a trust due to the tax-deferral of the charitable trust.

By weaving together the different elements of Wealth Management, Dr. Exit was able to use a charitable trust to help address a number of family goals, financial outcomes, and tax-saving strategies, leaving a more substantial financial legacy. His goal was to set his kids up so they would be even better off than he was, but in the process not let wealth destroy them.

Those are the conversations we're having with our clients. Dr. Exit was on board: "I'm set. I want to be a good steward of this. I want to increase my impact even more now." Some questions clients ask me are:

- How do I pay less in taxes, Tim?

- How do I have more of an impact?

- How do I build a lasting legacy?

- How do I have meaningful legacy conversations with my kids?

- How do I teach my kids to give and not be wasteful with their money?

One of the things that came into play with Dr. Exit was discussing the importance of the time involved to set this up. Perhaps you are wondering how quickly you can accomplish all of your gifting goals?

A timeless Chinese Proverb states, *"The best time to plant a tree was twenty years ago. The second best time is now."*

The same is true with Charitable Gifting.

We can implement some strategies in less than an hour. Some take weeks or months to fully implement. However, what can always be done immediately is **The Dental Wealth Nation Unlimited Discovery Process**™.

For example, I was speaking with Dr. Middle of Career on December 24, 2020. He had heard Russ Alan Price and me speak to his Mastermind group about Elite Wealth Planning a month earlier. At this point, Dr. MOC was not a client. He did not have an account with me. We'd had a couple of conversations, and then we came to the end of the year. He said, "I've had a fantastic year! What can be done with my extra profits?" We then started talking about that value piece, especially with his kids. I brought that up because I knew that was important to him. How did I know? Because I had been asking questions about the seven key drivers of success (more to come in the next chapter) and constant discovery. We could find more components that were valuable to him.

That's one of the good things an advisor always does. If your advisor is not always pushing in and asking questions, you'd better find another advisor. If they're telling more than they're asking, run away.

I'm in constant discovery.

Even if someone is not even a client yet, I already know all these details because of the constant discovery I do, even during a consult.

When we got to the end of the year, I knew it was important for Dr. Middle Of Career to create generational wealth to support the kids. It was also important for him to spend more time with the kids. It was clear he was charitable. He wanted to give back. I knew he had a good income, and he could do something meaningful with it.

This led me to bring up the idea of a Donor-Advised Fund.

Within a couple of days, we had the Donor-Advised Fund set up. We had funded it with $50,000 just a couple of days before the end of the year, and we saved him $25,000 in taxes.

While that was extremely beneficial to him, it wasn't the most important part. The most important part was now he had his Donor-Advised Fund that allowed him to sit down with his kids and say, "Hey, son. I've got a pool of money that I have set aside that's not mine, so we get to give it away."

We get to have an impact. It will not hurt our family. We are now prepared.

- What is important to you?
- Tell me about what causes you want to support?
- Let me teach you how beneficial it is to give money away and help worthy causes.

One way that we're instilling those values into his kids is by having discussions about charity, giving, and generosity—instead of hoarding.

It's showing your kids, through some proper planning, that you get to give money away! And there's no greater feeling in the world than giving money away. When you've earmarked money, specifically for charitable intent, it changes everything.

I don't know about you, but I usually find it a pain when people come to my door, or I get letters in the mail, regarding the fundraisers going on. Yes, it's great, and they're all for noble causes. Sometimes, you just feel like saying, "Here we go again. Someone's asking for money." Do you feel the same way as I do?

After I set up a Donor-Advised Fund for myself, people showed up again asking for money, like they always do. This time, my mindset shifted. "Oh, you know what? I'm so glad you're here. I've set aside money for this. Let me help you." I had planned for it. No longer did it feel like it was an intrusion. It became an opportunity.

Wouldn't you like that too? I know I want that for you, too, and I am confident you can get there.

Normally, when you give in the traditional way, you go in thinking, *This money isn't mine. It's theirs.* This is the mindset that some may have when they donate because it's already dedicated to their choice of foundation, charity, etc. What you'll see with the Donor-Advised Fund is that you still have all the control.

When you donate money to a Donor-Advised Fund, it goes out of your estate. It's an irrevocable gift, so you cannot get the funds back. You cannot use them for personal expenses. Why? Because you've gotten that tax deduction. You've given the money away.

Usually, when you give something away, you lose any ability to control it or direct it. If I give you $50,000, and then I tell you how to spend it, I really didn't give you $50,000. But one of the cool things about a Donor-Advised Fund is when you put the money in there, you still maintain some control over the funds.

- You get to say *who* it goes to.
- You get to choose *when* it goes to them.
- You get to choose *how* to invest the funds.
- You maintain control.
- You get an immediate tax deduction.

If your goal is to leave your favorite university or your favorite charity a major gift when you pass away, this is something you can put a little money into over time. You never have to give any money from the fund until you actually pass away. Or if you love giving a little money all throughout your life, you can put one of these together and give that way too. This is just one of the many ways to give and still maintain control with some strings attached, but you get to have that completed gift done. There really is a minimal downside to this. It's an irrevocable action, but again, *you* maintain control.

How does it sound to you so far?

- You get to give the funds.
- You get to *choose where* it goes.

- You get to *choose the timing* of the gifts, the *amounts* of the gifts, and the investments.

Now, the only thing you *can't* do is take it back and spend it on yourself.

Here's a concept to consider. Take a peek into Benjamin Hardy's book, *Willpower Doesn't Work*. He talks about just that. For example, if you try to set aside a pool of money for charity, and you *can* get it back, chances are you'll spend it on yourself. However, if you give it away, it's outside; it's earmarked and assigned to give. So you can bet it's going to go to the right places because you can't spend it on yourself anymore.

This is so powerful, and the power is in *your* hands.

Donor-Advised Funds Fees

As you've read, and maybe to your surprise, setting up your Donor-Advised Fund could take anywhere from a couple of days to a couple of weeks. By now, you're wondering how much it costs to set up. *Okay, Tim, what is the fine print on additional fees? I know it can't be that simple.* It's not as difficult as you might think, and the fees are certainly lower than you might expect.

What are the fees actually going to cost?

- It's going to depend on the institution you go to.
- It's going to depend on what investments you pick.
- It's going to depend on the advisor you work with.

In short, all the fees are super reasonable. It's very low cost in terms of the value received. Simply, it's the initial investment to set up, and the fee with the fund you choose. That's it!

When compared to the cost of a private foundation, the costs are minimal. Not just the cost with the administrative burden, but the administrative burden of running your own foundation versus doing a Donor-Advised Fund—very inexpensive. However, as I shared in Chapter 1 on Investment Consulting, products and investments in my industry are commoditized.

Who Are You?

Let's look at Dr. DIY again, a successful dental entrepreneur. One day, she reads an Internet article and comes across the concept of a Donor-

Advised Fund. She realizes, "Oh, my gosh! I don't have to do all this work to set up a foundation. I can set up a Donor-Advised Fund."

Eager to move forward, she sets up her own account, funds it, and now sh's ready to go. Through her journey, she is doing some gifting, but what she doesn't realize is she's missing some things. Namely, she didn't coordinate with her entire team.

Now she missed out on the fact that her income was actually much higher than she thought, and she could have put a lot more money in the Donor-Advised Fund and received a bigger write-off, allowing her to have a bigger impact.

Unfortunately, because she never had a holistic financial plan, she didn't know how much she could contribute to the fund, and it affected her lifestyle. She didn't have any guidance and therefore missed out on some big opportunities.

Whereas her friend, Dr. Middle of Your Career (MOC) whom she raved about the fund, said, "Oh, yeah! I set one of those up too. I used my Virtual Family Office to do it. They were able to build a coordinated gifting strategy. Now we're putting money in every single year. We've actually come up with a strategy for how to do this."

Dr. MOC's strategy was not haphazard; it was methodical.

This ties back into the drivers of an optimized financial world. One key thing is you want to move from doing things haphazardly to doing things methodically. The answer may seem obvious, but look at what it cost Dr. DIY not having a Virtual Family Office in place—a negative impact.

The tax impact is tremendous.

As a result of trying it herself, you can see the impact differential Dr. MOC was able to make versus Dr. DIY, who took the haphazard approach. Having a Virtual Family Office team can make such a difference, not just financially but regarding impact and legacy as well. Which trajectory would you prefer?

Private Family Foundation and Life Insurance

Another important option to introduce is the Private Family Foundations, private foundations, or family foundations. These interchangeable names are similar to nonprofit, tax-exempt organizations that make grants to charitable organizations. These allow the founder to control the management of the funds and what charities receive the gifts. A Private Family Foundation is overseen by a board of directors, which is often made up of family members, friends, and other advisors who help make all the major decisions about the foundation. While a Donor-Advised Fund is relatively simple and inexpensive to set up, a Private Family Foundation often has very significant legal startup and high ongoing management costs.

Summary of Charitable Gifting

Let me recap the five primary concerns of every client I meet with because I am sure you will relate to them:

1. You want to make good investment choices and smart decisions.

2. Tax mitigation is key because you never want to pay more than your fair share.

3. You want your assets (your money) to provide for the next generation and for the people you care about the most.

4. You will always be working on protecting everything you've worked so hard for from being unjustly taken in some kind of way. Whether that's lawsuits, divorce, or some other unjust means.

5. Since you are reading this, you are likely in the group who are very charitably inclined (one-third of the population) and want to have a lasting impact.

Tim & Dana's Legacy

When you're getting ready to exit, it's even more paramount to have your house in order. Let me share my personal story with you because I have experienced these concerns in my own life.

My wife and I were thinking more about our legacy and what it would look like. The truth is, thinking about our impact and our legacy is hard work.

For us, it's been a little bit like watching an old polaroid picture develop. Perhaps you remember the instant cameras first introduced decades ago. You take a photo and out pops the paper, but there is nothing on it at first glance. As you wait, the photo slowly develops until you have the full picture.

That is what legacy planning has been like for us. We still don't have all the details, but we are watching our picture develop.

At this point, we envision one day having a delightful piece of property with several acres where we can hold retreats for people to receive mental health counseling or provide help for kids with trauma. That dream is still taking shape.

Well, we don't know exactly what it's going to be right now, but we envision a center where people can come and have a safe place to heal, work on themselves, get better, and figure out what their impact will look like.

As we were thinking about that, our plans had always been, "Hey, when we pass away, we'll just give the money to charity." However, the more we thought about it, we realized, "We're going to have a pretty sizable estate by then, so we can probably head toward starting a self-supporting foundation that will last in perpetuity."

The more we thought about, it I said, "We'll have enough income to hire people to run this long after we're gone. That way, after we've left the planet, it'll really be a gift that keeps giving."

For us, it's not so much about *if* we are going to give; it's about our choices and *how* we want to do it continually. We don't have a Private Family Foundation. We don't have our vision fully developed, and we don't have all the details. We have learned to wait patiently while our picture develops.

However, just because we don't have a complete picture does not mean that we have not taken action on creating this future. We currently have a Donor-Advised Fund that we contribute to regularly. The amazing thing is that when we do form our Private Family Foundation, our Donor-Advised Fund can make a gift to the foundation.

It's a way for us to take action today, even without a fully formed plan. This is something you can do too. Don't let an imperfect picture of the future stop you from working toward what is most important to you.

Remember, it's about legacy.

Your legacy.

When you give and you support others, you are doing something that's authentic to yourself and who you are based on your unique gifts and abilities.

It's not just a one-and-done. By doing this, you'll be able to nudge the world in a way that you've made a lasting impact.

What are the foundations and charities that you want to stand for?

Lead with Your Superpower

I love my church. I love being there, but the idea of me serving the church by being the greeter or being the parking lot attendant . . . Well, I don't feel that's playing to my strengths in my wheelhouse.

Now, not that I'm above that kind of serving. If they needed someone to do that, I'd say, "Sure, I'll do those things."

However, those services do not highlight my unique gifts and abilities. There are people who absolutely love to stand out front and greet people, but that's not my gig.

I love serving through leading Financial Peace University classes and teaching people how to better manage their money. How do you make better choices? How do you affect the next generation?

When you're looking at giving, whether it's your time or resources, I encourage you to do what really aligns with the unique abilities that you're blessed with, that you're passionate about, and that showcase how you want to make a difference.

In that way, it's natural because you're just being you—instead of trying to fit into a mold somewhere.

Has there been a moment in your life when you thought, *Well, should I do the bake sale?* Or was something else nagging at you, and baking wasn't your best skill, but you still desired to serve?

Your heart is in the right place, but do you want to just fill in a gap? God has blessed us all with our own unique talents and abilities.

Lead with What You're Good At

Do what you're naturally gifted at. Do what you love because otherwise, you're going to be doing those other things and be miserable. Lead with your superpower.

You may think, *"All these rich people are just giving away their money. They never want to spend the time."* Time is the most precious resource.

Let me back up and first say that your faith and how you view the world is going to affect how you view money. Religion, faith, worldview—all of that has an impact.

As a Bible-believing Christian, I have typically served by giving money because I see myself as a steward of what God has given me. With giving, I love what one of my favorite pastors, John Piper, says: "When it comes to giving, you've got three kinds of Christians. You've got those who go out there and do the work. You've got those who give to support the work. And then you've got disobedient."

If your gifts and talents are working in a business and earning more income in a year than many people make in a lifetime (there are lots of people like that!), that's not a bad thing. God has gifted you with that ability, and you're good at it. Your role is probably better served to support and give; whereas other people have more time than money. They're going to be better off serving and getting in there and doing the hands-on stuff.

It takes everyone's contributions. Even with enough help, it's pretty hard to maintain the church if you can't afford it. Likewise, having a pile of money to pay for it but no volunteers isn't the best either.

In the same vein, I don't think you should give without some kind of involvement. I think there's an importance to being involved in the causes you support, whether that's talking with the people involved, knowing what's going on, or making friends in the organization.

You certainly want to do those things; you don't just want to write the check and disappear. They depend on you, not just for the monetary support, but the emotional support. They need someone to talk to, so be a mentor to them. Show them that you really care in all aspects.

I don't think there is a hard-and-fast rule as to the right or wrong way of giving. If you're doing it, then that's what's right. If you're not, I would make a case that this would be the exception to the rule and that you should look at changing it.

In concluding the Advanced Planning, ask yourself:

What Is *Your* Superpower?

By now, I hope you not only feel inspired but empowered. It is my firm belief that Charitable Gifting can change the future of your business and personal life. Do you relate more to Dr. DIY or Dr. Middle of Your Career? Are you curious about your current trajectory and how you might be able to further optimize your financial world?

I hope you're loving this more and more as we move along because that was all the setup to dive deep into Client Relationship Management. Yes, this includes the discovery process I promised you earlier. Here we go.

Client Relationship Management

Chapter 6

"Your goals are the only ones that matter."

C lient Relationship Management has two parts. First, it means building and fostering client relationships over time through the consultative discovery process. I've said many times, "It all starts with discovery!"—*because it does*. Second, Relationship Management involves managing other professional advisors—*both the ones in your network and new ones you may add*—in order to address advanced planning concerns. I'll elaborate on both parts in this chapter and then go further in Chapter 7.

Let's begin by restating the Wealth Management Formula because a successful client relationship is woven into this equation:

Wealth Management =
Investment Consulting + Advanced Planning + Relationship Management

Here we have the Relationship Management component, of the Wealth Management Formula, and this is where Client Relationship Management fits its piece into the rest of the bigger puzzle.

RM = CRM + PNRM
(Relationship Management) =
Client Relationship Management + Professional Network Relationship Management

Discovery

Successful Client Relationship Management starts and continues in discovery. That's the upper test for your advisor.

- Are they always doing discovery?
- Are they asking you substantial and thorough questions?
- Do they allow you to talk and carry the conversation? Or do they interrupt at some point and begin talking instead of gathering information?

You want an advisor who's always asking questions. One who is curious and listens to your unique life situations. Each question should become a diving-off point to ask more questions.

When I set an initial discovery meeting, it typically lasts about ninety minutes. Out of the full ninety minutes, the client is probably talking for about seventy minutes, and I'm spending about twenty minutes of the meeting asking questions.

Just like everything else in life. The 80/20 rule applies here too. So if your advisor is talking 80 percent of the time and you're only talking 20 percent of the time, then you'd better find another advisor. You want an advisor who actually cares and lets *you* talk 80 percent of the time.

In a discovery meeting with one of my clients, I said, "Do you realize that in just two meetings, you can have a picture of what everything looks like? We can do this so quickly." I followed that with, "Quick results require only two meetings, then you're done. Afterward, you'll know exactly what to do."

This is what I want to do for you.

Discovery encourages the human element, which is essential to a successful outcome. Client Relationship Management is the driving force behind the human element. It requires focusing on what's important to you, the client. The key feature is that the focus shifts from *products* to *personal solutions*.

Many professionals—financial, legal, and accounting—are hyper-focused on their particular area of expertise. Sure, they are fantastic at doing that *one* thing, but their thinking and strategy likely only revolves around that one thing.

They've got a hammer, and you're the nail.

If you've ever worked with a Wealth Manager, chances are the first thing that comes out of their mouth is, "Tell me about your assets.

Tell me about your liabilities. What financial problem do you want to solve?" Doesn't that sound familiar? They're putting the finances first instead of putting the human element first. Which do you prefer?

How does the human element really come into play during the discovery process if you are not the main focus? First, let me define the human element as "the personal and emotional component of Elite Wealth Planning." The human element is all about you. It's not simply a retirement plan or Captive Insurance company. It's not even a tax plan, tactic, or strategy. Ultimately, the human element is about helping you thrive even more in an uncertain socio-economic world.

The cornerstone of the human element always comes back to asking great questions. In fact, the reason the first meeting of the **Dental Wealth Nation Wealth Management Process**™ is called the discovery meeting is because we want to discover what's most important to you.

- Why do you care about retirement planning?
- Why do you care about protecting your family from risk?
- What's really going on in your financial world?
- What actually matters to you in the long term?
- Why do you care about keeping more money in your pockets? Is it because you want to support the causes and people that are important to you now, securing the future of your loved ones and the organizations who represent your values?

Do you see how it's really moving beyond the products into the personal solutions that are custom-built for you? Over the last decade, I've developed questions on seven key focus areas that dictate one's success in wealth. I'm about to share with you a sample of the foundational questions that I ask in a discovery meeting. You can access these questions and additional resources from: www.DentalWealthNationBook.com.

By having regular discovery meetings and aligning what we find with my process allows us to build out your total client profile—*that most others don't even attempt*—using The Virtuous Cycle.

Keep in mind that as we review these questions with you, this is just a small part of the wealth management process there's a larger cycle we follow called The Virtuous Cycle, which I'll share with you now.

The Virtuous Cycle

The Virtuous Cycle is a seven-step process of gathering information, looking for the best support system, mapping out options, then putting what you learn into action.

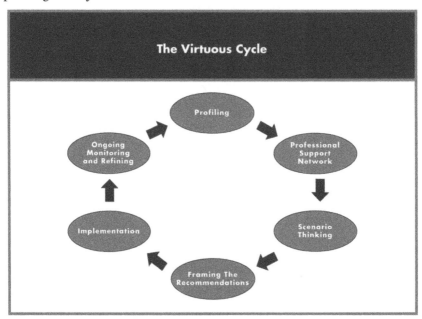

Profiling

Profiling asks four main questions:

- What is most important to you?
- What are your values?
- What are your goals?
- What do you hope to achieve?

Once we've established a clear picture of you and what you're working toward, then we seek the services of our professional support network.

Professional Support Network

This is a vetted team of some of the best in the industry to do what we call scenario thinking. There is no super genius. There's no one person you can depend on when delivering the highest-quality advice.

No one is a master of all the different aspects of specialized planning that are out there. There's no one who is an expert in everything. That's where the professional support network comes in. There's no one expert, but there are multiple experts in different fields. The world is too complex; there are too many things to know. Just like in the Dental field, you've got a whole bunch of different specialists. The same is true in Wealth Management. The general dentist may be able to do bits of prosthodontics, bits of perio, and bits of oral surgery. But when it really comes to something complex, you're going to send your patient to the oral surgeon. This requires you to have a support network of other specialists. The same is true with Elite Wealth Planning. Your Elite Wealth Planner is certainly going to be able to help you address a lot of your big concerns, but they're also going to have a very strong support network. That professional support network is invaluable for bringing in the experts you need, because a true Elite Wealth Planner knows they don't know everything, and they're not going to pretend like they do.

Scenario Thinking

In scenario thinking, we run through different strategies and tactics to see which ones will work the best. Playing out a possibility before committing to it can save time and money in the future.

Framing the Recommendations

The next step of the Virtuous Cycle is framing the *recommendations*, which means the recommendations are presented in a way that makes sense to the client via analogies and real-life situations from other clients. Things get explained in a way that actually makes sense. The end result is a client who says, "Oh, yeah! *This* is what I'm doing!"

Implementation

Once you frame the recommendations, it's time to do the nitty-gritty of actually implementing the plan. Even the most well-thought-out plans are useless if they are never put into action.

Ongoing Monitoring and Refining

The next phase of the cycle is ongoing monitoring and refining. You always want to be updated. You always want to be looking at the plan. Life is like a perpetual movie, not a snapshot, and things are always changing. That's why you want to continue to follow the virtuous cycle.

For each one of these steps I could write a whole chapter. Honestly, I could write a whole book, *and what do ya know? now I have!* So let me just give you a brief example of how one of these important elements, Scenario Planning comes into play.

Let's return to Dr. VFO, a doctor whom I worked with. Dr. VFO was a couple of years out from his liquidity event—*selling his business.*

When we were doing Scenario Thinking, we ran through these different strategies.

- What happens if he sells the business outright?
- What happens if he sells the business to another DSO (dental support organization) who takes over and moves you into management?
- What does an employee stock option purchase plan look like?
- What happens if he sells the company to your employees?

While going through these different scenarios, we came across a situation where Dr. VFO has owned the building for over twenty years, so there is potential real estate income. That was actually one of the biggest concerns for this doctor. It was a massive piece of real estate, potentially generating $400,000 to $500,000 a year in net income. Wouldn't you say that's a pretty marvelous piece of real estate? He not only owned the real estate, but his dental practice was 100 percent housed in the building! Now we're left wondering, *What if he sells the practice to a DSO, or another dentist, and the buyer runs it into the ground? What happens now with his biggest tenant?* Gone.

When you are involved in any transition, you have a lot of interconnected pieces. Scenario Planning looks at how these pieces are connected and how they impact each other. Imagine selling your dental practice only to lose your biggest tenant and, subsequently, your real estate income from the business. This is really something you would want to uncover ahead of time, just like Dr. VFO did.

You may think, *What if he just sold the building outright?* Fair question; the building would be worth five or six million dollars. However, now you have to deal with taxes. A traditional solution would be to sell the building and do a 1031 Exchange to avoid taxes. But that in and of itself creates an issue because now you've got to worry about finding a replacement property. You've still got the tenant problem, and now you've got a management problem. That doesn't necessarily sound like a fun retirement, at least it didn't for Dr. VFO.

Through the process of Scenario Planning, we've been exploring selling the building to a real estate investment trust that will come in, buy the building, and then through the process build him a diversified portfolio of real estate that he doesn't have to manage. With this approach, he will still get his potential $500,000 a year cash flow. It's a perfect solution for him—without the risk of a single tenant.

You can't take a "one size fits all" approach to selling. Again, one of the great things about the Scenario Planning process is we can constantly take different approaches to find the best solutions. The mindset behind Scenario Planning is, *What happens if?* This, of course, happens hand in hand with the Professional Support Network.

For Dr. VFO, we then brought in retirement planning experts to optimize how much money he could put into his retirement plan. We also brought in business transition specialists.

Scenario Planning requires getting real numbers. It's one thing for you and I to talk theoretically about how something may work for you. It's another thing to put real numbers to your plan so that you actually see what it means for you.

The other thing we want to look at is your after-tax net. One of the original private equity groups was going to pay Dr. VFO close to $21 million. While that amount is a pretty nice valuation, there is still a little problem called taxes. His after-tax net would be about half of the twenty-one million.

The tax issue was one reason we started to look at an employee stock option plan because by selling it to the employees via an ESOP trust, he'd get a higher after-tax return.

Let's say Dr. VFO sells to an ESOP and profits $18 million instead of $21 million. Well, is that more money? Yes, the net after-tax result is significantly higher because ESOPs get favorable tax treatment. These are all the things that go into scenario thinking, and a Professional Support Network serves as the expert in all these strategies. It's impossible to maximize your profits without one in place.

That's just a quick example of how Scenario Planning comes into play. However, Scenario Planning won't work unless we really understand you and what's important to you.

One of the ways the Ultra-Wealthy get fantastic results is that they follow this process instead of doing things haphazardly. Once you accomplish all the steps in the Virtuous Cycle, then you're right back to profiling. There is a model that only the most sought-after Elite Wealth Planners at the top of their game use. It's the model I use. It lives within the profiling step and is called The Total Client Model.

The Total Client Model

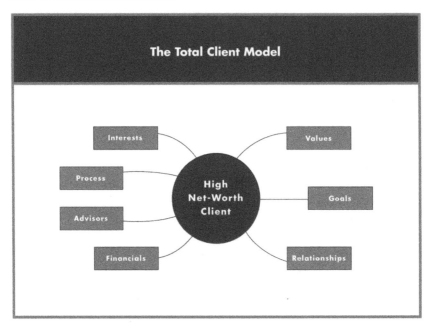

In the Total Client Model, we really dive in and profile around seven key areas, placing *you* at the center. We're asking about your values, your goals, and your most important relationships. Simply put, if you're not doing constant discovery, you're not optimizing your financial world.

VALUES

The following questions help define your values:

- Make a list of what is most important to you.
- What drives your beliefs about money?
- What experiences have shaped your perspective on money?
- What does financial success mean to you?

GOALS

Identifying your goals provides clarity and focus:

- What are you trying to achieve with your money—now and in the future? Make sure your goals are realistic yet challenging enough so you build your faith in the process.

- Create timelines for specific goals: short-term, mid-term, and long-term. Making your goals time-bound is key for success.

- What impact do you want your money to have on those you love and the causes you value?

RELATIONSHIPS

People are wired to connect and to care for one another. The family unit is where relationship bonds are typically the strongest, but not always. This is why it's important to assess your unique circle of people.

- Identify the important relationships in your life.

- Identify the most important *family* relationships.

- Who will benefit from your successful Wealth Management now and when you are gone?

- What legacy do you want to leave behind for those who know and love you?

Are there any parents or relatives that you're supporting or taking care of? Often, the answer is, "Oh yeah! I've got a sister that I'm helping to support," or "I've got some parents back home in another country, and I'm sending them money every single month to help support them." Those are important things to know and understand because if something happens to you, it's not just affecting you and your immediate family here; it's also affecting your family overseas as well. Only after we identify the information held within your values, goals, and relationships can we finally start talking about the financial part. We don't place our initial focus on the financials because we want to know what drives your actions every day. What is motivating you to create wealth and use it to the best of your ability?

FINANCIALS

What types of vehicles should you be leveraging? The financials empower you to take care of your goals and your relationships, not the other way around. When we do a thorough analysis on financials, we are focused on three main things:

- We're looking at how assets are held.
- We're looking at what you actually own.
- We're looking at what you owe.

With the answers you provide, we see how it all fits together.

ADVISORS

Maybe you've got a great team, or maybe we've got to look at throwing in a replacement here or there. Who are the professionals you're working with? How do you feel about these relationships?

- Who is managing your money?
- Who is your CPA?
- Who is your accountant?
- Who is your attorney, both personal and business?
- Who are the insurance professionals you are working with?

Then, we dive in and look at the process.

PROCESS

- How do you prefer to work with advisors?
- Do you want to be hands-on?
- Do you want to be part of every decision-making process?
- Do you prefer someone to say, "Hey, here's the recommendations, and here's the one-hundred-page document. We did our research, but you just need this

one page?" Or are you the type who wants the one-hundred pages?

INTERESTS

Here, we come full-circle by identifying what you enjoy when you are *not* working!

- What do you like to do when you're not working?
- What does an ideal vacation look like to you?
- What are your interests?
- What are the causes you support?
- How do you have fun?
- How do you rest and relax?

The Total Client Model provides a deep understanding of what's important in your world, who the professionals are, and how we can move forward.

By the way, this is a real document, not just some random list on a scratchpad. As another gift to you, I've added it for you to download in the Resources section to help you visualize what yours may look like.

When I'm talking to my clients, I'm always updating and asking questions about these themes. I'm making notes and changing the document as things change. Life is always changing, and you want to respond to what changes in your world.

Dr. Exit's Early Days

Let's look at how The Total Client Profile changed Dr. Exit's future early on. When Dr. Exit was only forty-nine years old, he had built a very successful multi-location, practice—three locations and working on opening his fourth. He has two great kids and a great marriage. He enjoys supporting the community, taking care of people, and wants to give his kids a head start in life. He also wants to spend more time with his family. He once again got approached by a group looking to buy the practice and started going down that road.

He had done a little planning but nothing in-depth. And so we started by discovering some major risks that were in his retirement plan. He had something set up called a *pooled plan*, meaning that everyone's money was all in one pot. The employees didn't get to choose how to invest their own funds; the doctor was taking full responsibility for investing everyone's funds. We helped him clean things up and work on the transition piece so that by the time he finally sold, he was able to walk away with $7 million in the bank and an even more substantial piece of "back end" equity. When it was all done, he felt like a big weight had been lifted off his shoulders.

The Total Client Profile supported his success. He was able to enter his future with confidence and peace of mind. He didn't want to cash out completely. But he took enough money off the table so he could set up his family for life, enabling him to leave a thriving legacy.

Now that he has exited, one of the key things we've focused on is keeping him healthy.

I always tell people, "Everything's okay until it's not."

The beautiful thing about all the planning we had done together is that Dr. Exit and his family are going to be okay, no matter what. In fact, one of the things that I've turned Dr. Exit onto is a concierge medical professional.

Concierge Medicine

I'm a huge proponent of *concierge medicine*. A concierge medical doctor is a medical professional that you can have on retainer. You pay them for advice, but not only when you get sick. With this specialty service, you're compensating a doctor now to keep you healthy, instead of paying them when you get sick. I'm a huge fan of concierge doctors, and I think this is another great asset to have as part of your team. I have been recommending concierge doctors for the last ten years.

In the Virtual Family Office world, this is commonplace for very wealthy families. They have doctors on retainer because they travel the world. They'll take that emergency medical kit with them that has everything. The use of concierge doctors among the Ultra-Wealthy and those with single-family offices has been growing for years. According to AES Nation, 61.4 percent of single-family offices now make use of concierge medical services. If you hire a concierge doctor, you're paying them to keep you healthy, and that's a way better equation.

We implemented that for Dr. Exit. We also helped him merge accounts that were all over the place. They probably had eight different accounts across four different financial institutions, and we got them down to three accounts at one firm. Consolidation and simplicity.

We then worked on reviewing their medical power of attorney and updating their trust once they sold the practice.

Now that they're retired, this charitable gift is really going to become a much bigger piece for them because now they've got additional time to do this and pursue those things that are important to them.

If you're interested in diving deeper into concierge doctors, I've got a book recommendation dedicated to that called *The World of Concierge Medicine: How a Renaissance in Health Care Can Help You and Your Loved Ones Live Long and Healthy* by Russ Allan Prince.

Dental Wealth Nation Wealth Management Process™

Time is precious to you, and when your time is up, no matter how much money you have, you can't buy more days on Earth. So how long does it take to start this process? First, the Discovery Meeting happens. Two weeks later, we'll get together for an Investment Plan Meeting to give you ideas on how to move forward. A week later, we'll do the Mutual Commitment Meeting.

The only decision I ever ask a potential client to make in our first meeting is this: "Are we going to have a second meeting?" Sometimes clients are ready to get started right away and say, "Let's sign paperwork!" I respond with, "This is too big of a decision. I want you to read through the details, then talk to your spouse. Bring me your questions because you should have a lot!"

There's zero pressure in the Investment Plan Meeting to make any kind of final decision because these are major life choices. I want to relieve all that so that you can fully analyze the plan. If we have to make some tweaks, adjustments, and changes, that's what that meeting is for. At the Mutual Commitment Meeting is where we—together—make a choice if we want to work together or not.

The reality is that you can have a plan in place and get started in less than a month. From there, we will continue to fine-tune deeper strategies and continue to implement and respond to the changes that take place in your life.

Speed of implementation is another added benefit of a Virtual Family Office. When you come into higher levels of wealth, people want to work with the best professionals around. I believe as you're reading this, you do too. Geographic location isn't a barrier as long as you're getting the top-notch, customized care you need for your personal and business finances.

You can bring in the best people for your situation, no matter what city or country they live in. A lot of times you may not have the best people for what you're trying to achieve in the city or town you live in. Maybe you're choosing from mediocre local professionals, or maybe you've got some really great professionals nearby, but they don't understand your industry as well as they ought to. That's the power of going digital.

We live in a world that's so used to *digital* these days—avatars, icons, and entrancing or distracting videos. I think many people get lost in the noise and forget what it means to actually be *connected* to other human beings.

When I help my clients, I want to focus on their individual needs. It's very important that we have a face-to-face meeting. Sometimes that can't happen in person. The technology we have today can help support our business needs. Even if we are working digitally, we are doing *real* work. We are connecting live and working together to help you achieve your goals.

So whether you are across the US or in the same city as me, I want to make sure you get the same value of meeting no matter where you are. While 98 percent of my business *is* made up of dentists, I will go outside of this field when the opportunity arises and if I can legitimately help someone. Why? Because I'm in the business of helping.

When I had a fifty-seven-year-old local business owner come to me for help, I gladly obliged. He's probably worth $24 million, but was outside of my typical dentistry clientele. I wanted to help him though. I met him years ago at a community event where I was speaking. We talked about strategies to become super wealthy, and he wanted to learn more about what the Ultra-Wealthy are doing.

During my presentation, I talked about maximizing retirement plans and contributions. Retirement plan contributions are one of the biggest advantages that you have as a business owner to maximize your wealth, and it is so underutilized.

This local business owner had a simple IRA in place, and he was maxing it out. The limits on the *simple* IRAs are very low. We talked about doing a defined benefit plan and getting him about ten times the contribution he was getting in the simple IRA.

I also pointed out a massive tax deduction he could take, and how he could put away more funds on a pretax basis and keep more money in his pocket. Eventually, he decided, "Man, I want to do it, but I'm just not ready yet." How many times have you said the same? "I should have done it, but life kicked in, and I got busy."

He got busy. In fact, I didn't hear from him for a while, despite me reaching out. Suddenly, he called me about three years later: "Tim, I'm ready to do this. I just had an incredible year. I really should have done that three years ago because that would mean an extra $300,000 that I would have in the plan—without paying taxes on it. I'm ready to go now!"

I was ready to move him forward. We started looking at all the different illustrations and running scenarios. Doing that Scenario Planning and running illustrations with real numbers drew out the "how" of this plan. It's one thing to talk hypothetically about how these things work. It's a powerful thing to put into practice.

My main concern for him was: "How does this work for you? How does this work for your business, your situation, and what you're trying to achieve?"

We started looking at doing a benefit focus plan, which is where we can strive to get the most money in a plan. There are some commitments you have to make in terms of ongoing contributions. My client said, "I am really not comfortable with that level of contribution." We dialed the contribution levels down and ended up putting in place a 401(k) profit-sharing plan, maximized for him and his wife. We also coordinated with his CPA to make sure everything tied in together.

Not only did we run the illustration for one year, we also ran it looking at what his future workforce expected to look like. We wanted to make sure that the future pharmacist he hired sticks around. We actually optimized the plan to make sure that the future pharmacist will get a pretty nice chunk of change into the retirement plan. Doing this will help him keep a good employee and will attract future qualified employees.

What was his pain point? Solving the tax piece and putting the plan in place. We did that. Then we looked at the family-limited partnership that he had in place. We wanted to reanalyze that because he had done his planning incrementally—a little here, and then a little there. He'd never systematically looked at how all the puzzle pieces fit together.

With proper discovery in place, we really get to know what you want to achieve. That's the question you have to ask yourself: "Are my plans going to deliver as promised?"

- Will your Wealth Management Plan still be effective a decade or two from now?

- Is your insurance planning at the correct levels?

- Is your estate planning up to date?

That's why we go through and leave no stone unturned. However, we don't stop there. Another important element of discovery is stress testing.

Stress Test

While you may have been used to that advisor you've known since high school, the cost you wager could be millions, if not more, if you fail to run a stress test. One of the greatest examples of the impact of a stress test is shown in my personal story.

Early on, my wife was facing a disability, and the disability policy she had was not correct. She took out this policy before we met—bought it as soon as she got out of dental school. The policy was about fourteen years old before we realized her well-meaning advisor just didn't have the technical expertise to help her. We caught that error and made the correction.

Disability is a real issue for dentists. One in three dentists become disabled long enough to collect benefits at some point during their career. The next time you attend a CE meeting, look to your left, then look to your right. Then look at yourself, one of you is going to be disabled at some point in your career.

Imagine how you would feel if you'd been paying on a disability policy for fourteen years, and you reach a point where you say, "Holy moly! I may require a disability policy because I can't hold forceps to do extractions anymore in my practice." You begin seeing specialists, then look at the documents and determine, "Well, I'm so glad I got a disability policy I've been paying on for fourteen years." Then you find out that half of those benefits are going to disappear because some well-meaning advisor tried to get you a tax deduction because he was so focused on technical wizardry instead of the human element and what's really important.

I didn't know about stress testing then. All of a sudden, my wife was facing a potential disability. I remember saying to her, "Oh, hey, we should probably look at your disability policy and check this thing out." It was set up in a way that the benefits were fully taxable to her. Why was this taxable when it didn't have to be? Because her previous advisor had said, "Hey, why don't you pay for this disability policy through your dental practice, and you can get a tax deduction?" Well, that sounds like a great idea, except the problem is if you pay for the policy that way and ever need to go on disability, then that policy—when those benefits come to you—is 100 percent taxable as opposed to paying for the policy with after-tax dollars, in which you have tax-free income when you need it the most.

I want you to be equipped to avoid situations like this.

There are two primary reasons for considering running a stress test on your wealth plans.

- First, you want to avoid destructive situations and catch things before they happen.
- Second, you want to make sure you're taking advantage of all the opportunities that are out there for you.

The reason stress testing is so important, especially as your wealth grows, is the frequency of errors in your plan. You may have an auto policy that doesn't have high enough limits, or you may have never purchased an umbrella policy, or you need to update your beneficiaries on your IRA.

Typically, you will have more errors at lower net worth, but the cost and the impact of that error, because the dollar numbers are so much smaller, means that the severity of that error is pretty small. One percent of $1,000 isn't a lot of money. If you've got a little error, it's going to cost you something, but not that much.

As your wealth grows, the severity of the errors gets far more costly. Suddenly, you've got a couple of million dollars in the bank with a 1 percent error. Well, now, that's a costly error to you.

It's similar to the tax planning on the sale of the business we were talking about. If you sell a business for $20,000, your taxable effects are pretty minimal. You didn't really need to do any kind of planning. You sell a business for $20 million, and half of it disappears to taxes. That's a $10 million error.

That is the rationale behind stress testing. You want to catch those errors to make sure you're taking advantage of all the opportunities out there.

Stress testing is so important I have another gift for you. It relates directly to stress testing and the importance of second opinions. Visit *www.DentalWealthNationBook.com* to grab a copy of this resource.

Second Opinions

Today, we often look to multiple sources to make our final decisions about almost everything—from the cars we buy to the medical care we receive. Your financial future shouldn't be any different from the other advisors you seek.

There is an underlying theme around a lot of clients, and it usually starts with questions like, "How do I legally pay less in taxes?" If they're coming to me, I'm the advisor that they come to for that second opinion.

"What do I do? My existing team really doesn't know this stuff, and they don't know how to tie this all into my plan. I need a second opinion, Tim. What do we do?"

Usually, it always starts with a tax-planning piece. From there, I go to the easy opportunities: "Are you maximizing your retirement plan?" The answer is usually, "No, I don't know what that means."

When you want someone to tell you what's going on, then get a second opinion. Not all second opinions I've provided clients are the same. I've done second opinions before where I say, "You know what? You're in great shape. Just go back to your existing advisor and make this little tweak. You don't need to hire me. You're fine. God bless you. I'm glad I could help. Let me know if anything changes."

However, I would tell you that absolutely every single stress test is very similar in one regard. They typically all start with tax planning in some form or another or questions regarding transition. I've even had newer doctors that I've onboarded who say, "I don't need a second opinion. A first opinion is what I need. I've never even looked at this stuff."

Whether you need a second opinion or you're just getting started with the first, that's why I wrote this book for you, and I'm here to help.

My $1,500,000 Million Dollar Mistake

It's easy to make mistakes. Some you may not even know you're making until years later, myself included. I'd like to share with you how Hollywood Tower Records cost me one million five hundred thousand dollars.

When I was seventeen, I set up my first IRA and put some money in year one. In year two, I put additional money in. Year three, however, I had more important things to do. When you're nineteen, you want to spend time with your friends. For me, it meant going down to the record store and buying whatever the latest release was at Hollywood Tower Records.

Main point? I stopped putting money into my IRA.

I was thinking about it a couple of years ago: *I wonder what my IRA would be worth if I kept putting money into it.* Low and behold, the calculation I made came to over $1,500,000 dollars.

Aside from meeting my wife, there's not a single experience that I've had in the last thirty years that I would trade for an extra $1,500,000 in the bank. Your financial future is ALWAYS worth a second—*or first*—look.

Dr. Virtual Family Office: Origin Story

These days, I primarily work with DSOs, multi-practices owners, and multi-specialty owners. Early on in my career, however, there was a younger couple I was working with who were set to be in the position of Dr. VFO thirty years from now. They were well on their path to creating significant wealth. He was a specialist orthodontist with an established practice generating about $1.1 to $1.2 million dollars a year, and he wanted to continue to grow and provide for his family.

Their focus was retirement, their children's college—and they still wanted to buy their toys so they could jet ski and have fun on the lake. Both of them grew up living paycheck to paycheck, and they knew they didn't want that, especially for their kids. They wanted to provide their kids with opportunities. They wanted stability. They wanted to spend wisely, yet they still wanted to have fun.

No one wants a budget that you can't have any fun with. A budget should *give you freedom* to enjoy the things you want to do. Their biggest goals were building the practice, cutting back on controlled expenses, and offering benefits to their employees. They also wanted to support their parents as needed in the future without having to worry about making ends meet.

Regarding financial stability, they were concerned because they really weren't doing any savings at all for their future. They had their practice, but they didn't have any kind of retirement plan in place. When we did the assessment of their most important relationships, we found their marriage, their parents, and their kids were super important to them. They were also involved in their community as well, so they loved being helpful where they could.

They'd get referrals from their community, which is very important. Their church family played a major role in their lives, as well as from the schools their children attended. Did I mention they had a dog and a cat they absolutely saw as part of the family?

We did a full assessment of where their practice was. We got a valuation for them, did the data analysis, and did insurance analysis. We performed a deep, deep dive. Because they were newer in their career, they didn't have any will or trust in place. They had a collection of advisors, but no actual team. They loved getting out there and just having fun, taking vacations, attending sporting events, and supporting their kids' sports teams.

When we met, I got them set up with a qualified plan for their office and helped them put away over $75,000 a year on a pretax basis. They received a major tax deduction, and could now save for their future. Along the way, I met with their kids, and we've been able to set up retirement accounts for their children so that they can grow a financial security plan, then build from there when they enter the workforce. I don't want their kids making the same $1,500,000 mistake that I did.

Just like Dr. VFO, they were setting their kids up for financial success by doing some generational planning so *they wouldn't have to grow up living paycheck to paycheck like their parents did.* They're affecting the next generation.

I share that with you because the planning we did really came to fruition one day.

Imagine making the call to your advisor and telling them, "I just want to let you know that Dr. VFO just had a stroke. We don't know what we're going to do right now."

After listening to you share all those cares and concerns, you can say, "I just want to let you know how grateful we are that we've met you and that we could work with you. We're going through a terrible situation, and by working with you, it's a little less bad because we've got more financial stability. We know we have the right team around us who can help us survive this."

The rewarding part of what I do is adding some stability to people's lives. Again, just like my wife, my clients have prepared for these things.

They know, with some confidence and certainty, that they're not only going to be okay, but they're changing the course of generations. It's the Emotional Ripple Effect. I know how the story ends because I've seen it before. But in their case, their health issues hit earlier—not later.

They survived the health and business crisis because they had—*and still have*—the right team in place. We knew we had the right policies in place and were ready for it. They could thrive amidst uncertainty.

Emotional Ripple Effect Return On Investment

Dave Ramsey said, "The number one issue couples fight about is money." According to a survey by Ramsey Solutions, money fights are the second leading cause of divorce behind infidelity. When I help you add a little financial stability, a little confidence, and clarity around finances, we can build healthier marriages, healthier families, and leave a positive, lasting impact on your family and the ones you love.

$$RM = CRM + PNRM$$
(Relationship Management) =
Client Relationship Management + Professional Network Relationship Management

As a refresher in closing, the total client profile and Client Relationship Management are about your values and goals. It's all about selecting the right advisors, defining your process, and understanding your assets.

This is what I do one-on-one. It's the constant discovery process of focusing on what's important to you. Why do you want to do what you do, and how can we make it happen?

If you are serious about achieving those goals, you need a team of experts. No one's an expert in all the diverse areas that are out there. You need help with the advanced planning that we will soon discuss.

This is really where the Virtual Family Office comes in. I've been running my virtual Family Office for years, which is one of the many reasons I'm so passionate about helping you with yours.

This leads us to the second part of the Relationship Management Formula: professional network relationship management, the vetting process that we've talked about. It's bringing in the best of the best talent on a full-time or as-needed basis to your team of coordinated professionals to manage your wealth so that you can implement wealth enhancement, wealth transfer, wealth protection, and charitable gifting to further optimize your financial world.

Professional Network Relationship Management

Chapter 7

"It takes a coordinated team of professionals to manage your wealth."

I magine waking up to find out all your money is gone. At first, you think you are having a bad dream, seeing your financial advisor being arrested on TV. The same advisor whom you've been working with for years and has been giving you great returns on your money.

Unfortunately, it wasn't a dream but a real-life nightmare for many of Bernie Madoff's victims. Madoff was an American fraudster and financier who ran the largest Ponzi scheme in history, worth about $65 billion. Investors put their trust in him because he created a front of respectability. His returns weren't over the top, and he had people believing he implemented a legitimate strategy, called a "split-strike conversion," which, in fact, he did not. According to Justice.gov and CNBC, Madoff Investment Securities LLC (BLMIS) fraud scheme, Madoff's total distribution was over $3.7 billion to nearly 40,000 victims in 125 countries over four decades worldwide by the time Madoff was busted on December 11, 2008—after his two sons turned him in.

Madoff was by far the worst and biggest financial con artist in recorded history, but he's not the only one, nor will be the last.

Understanding that not everyone is honest or has your best interests at stake is detrimental when it comes to handling your money. Let me start by breaking down the character of the professionals who are out there working: the good, the bad, and the ugly. Remember, forewarned is forearmed.

Types of Professionals

Types of Professionals				
			Expertise Level	
			Low	High
Intended to Benefit	You		Pretender	Elite Wealth Planner
	Themselves		Predator	Predator / Exploiter

When it comes to different types of professionals, there are some dangerous ones to watch out for: the Pretender, the Predator, and the Exploiter. My assumption is you're not working with a Predator or an Exploiter, but you may encounter a Pretender. What exactly is a Pretender? Generally, this professional is a well-meaning advisor who likely has your best interests at heart. Pretenders are not bad people who are out to exploit you. But the problem with Pretenders is that they don't have the professional level of expertise to serve you well.

Pretenders

Pretenders want to do a good job—in the same way an amateur baseball player may want to hit those home runs—but they don't have the competence, proficiency, or experience to do it. I've encountered many financial advisors who are Pretenders. They got into the industry as a second career because they have a good way with people and know how to connect. But since the job isn't a calling or it's simply done for a paycheck, they don't always aim to be the best at what they do and lack the technical expertise to serve you well.

I could list dozens of industries in which I see Pretenders, such as real estate agents, insurance agents, investment advisors, accountants, and attorneys. Their career mindset looks like this: "I took my test and got my license. I'm ready to help someone! I know what I'm doing." Good for them at this starting-off point. But what these Pretender professionals fall prey to is the mindset of thinking they know everything, so they believe there is nothing left to learn. A good financial planner, or anyone who assists people with money, assets, and their well-being, should always be on top of the latest developments in their field and always focus on their client's needs above their own.

Predators

Next, let's move on to the Predators. These people are characterized by two main features. First, like Pretenders, they have a low level of technical expertise. Second, they are opportunists whose main concern is looking out for their bottom line. Predators are skilled at wowing you with a PowerPoint presentation, or even hosting a fabulous seminar dinner, but that's as far as their prowess goes. Their main goal is getting you in the door; after that, their focused client care abruptly ends.

Exploiters

The Exploiters are in a category all by themselves! For starters, these professionals have a very high level of technical expertise (think of them as the Bernie Madoff's of the world). Once again, they're out to benefit themselves. They don't care about you whatsoever. They want to pad their own pockets. But instead of doing it the Predator's way (bombarding you with attention, then offering breadcrumbs), these snakes intentionally manipulate you by creating false statements, wowing you with their (high-level) of technical knowledge, thus getting you to buy into a false sense of security and client care. Remember, Exploiters are only in business for themselves, not for you.

To complicate matters a bit, I will say that some Predators do fall into the category of being highly competent in their field, but you can easily filter them out from the Exploiters once you are able to determine their motivations. In my experience, most people do not work with Predators and Exploiters for long periods of time. Sure, they're out there, but they eventually get exposed. They exist for a season, then they're gone. But working with them for any amount of time can destroy your wealth management plan, your livelihood, and your family's future.

Most people, however, encounter and work with Pretenders frequently. Often, it's by choice—or rather an obligation. A Pretender might be the buddy you met in college, and you feel too guilty to make a change. You know this professional could (and should!) be doing more for you, but you don't want to burn any bridges or rock the boat by parting ways.

Perhaps your Pretender is the well-meaning financial adviser you've had for years who wants to work with you, but he doesn't have a high level of mastery, excellence, or proficiency to offer. Maybe it's your golfing buddy who personally solicited you in becoming your financial advisor. What about your friend at the country club, who pressured you into a business arrangement? If you'd have said no, it would be awkward seeing them every week after rejecting their services. Besides, you've had a good business relationship with them so far (just not great), and you have seen some results (but not what you had hoped for). Why change anything?

Well, for starters, what is this relationship costing you? Probably more than you realize! I know breaking up isn't easy, but may I remind you it's costing you a great deal of money right now, and even more over the years—especially over your lifetime.

When going through the stress test, there are things that we'll catch in your unique situation that have been overlooked. That's why the cost is so high. When you're overpaying in taxes, you're wasting time and not taking advantage of all the opportunities out there for you. Your hard work, which turns into money, is disappearing and going to the government instead of to the people you love and the causes you care about. It's also severely impacting your ability to change the world for the better. The longer you wait, the more money you stand to lose out on.

Wealth Planners vs. Elite Wealth Planners

What are the differences between Wealth Planners and *Elite* Wealth Planners? Whether your investable assets are a few million or tens of millions, the "technically adept" Wealth Planners and financial advisors heavily saturate the industry and represent themselves throughout the spectrum, so understanding what makes an Elite

Wealth Planner provide services over and above the basic Wealth Planner is only tricky if you don't inform yourself of what to expect from the best.

An Elite Wealth Planner will usually limit their clients to a small number of affluent families whom they know they can sufficiently inform and guide. You choosing from the two could mean the difference between being just another number—a transaction—versus being treated like a unique person, working with a professional who is carefully assessing your needs and goals, whose main aim is to help *you* succeed.

Comparing Wealth Planners and Elite Wealth Planners

Aspect	Technically Adept Wealth Planner	Elite Wealth Planner
Technical Expertise	State-Of-The-Art	State-Of-The-Art
Focus	Legal Strategies And Financial Products	The Human Element

Wealth Planner

A good Wealth Planner is going to have state-of-the-art expertise. In terms of a Wealth Planner's focus, they are going to be focused on the legal strategies, the financial products. They want to understand the technical wizardry behind what they do, even if it leaves out the human element. True, they are business savvy, but their focus is mainly on the product and the strategies they want to implement instead of going over and above to provide personal service and connection.

Elite Wealth Planner

When you move over to an Elite Wealth Planner, you get a high level of technical expertise. But the added feature is that the focus fundamentally shifts from products and services to what I mentioned earlier—the human element, focusing on what's most important to you (the client) and not trying to wow you with technical wizardry. Elite Wealth Planners listen carefully. They are determining what's important to you! Products and services are matched up according to what these professionals find in your connection and conversation because *they are listening.*

Questions to ask a potential Elite Wealth Planner:

- Are your strategies and financial products legal?

- Do you focus on the human element?

- How do your strategies and plans in the short-term connect in the long-term?

- How do your services benefit me, the client?

- What are you going to do that's in the best interest of my family?

- What makes you different from the other Elite Wealth Planners out there?

Imagine sitting down with a professional, and the first thing he says to you is, "Hey, check out all these cool products and services. Which ones do you like?" As you're sitting there, you're probably wondering, *Well, I'm not really sure what each of these do for me.* You may reluctantly pick something he randomly suggests because he's the professional and must know what he's doing, right?

Would you feel confident leaving that meeting? I'm sure you wouldn't. Why? Because the human element is missing. That one-on-one human conversation.

Who Can You Trust?

How do you find these Elite Wealth Planners? Well, this is where a vetting process comes in. Let me share with you how I determine who I trust and promote and how I vet other Elite Wealth Planners. There are several things you want to look at when working with any professional because there are Pretenders, Predators, and Exploiters lurking about. Are you wondering, *How do I know who to trust?* Well, one of the things you want to examine is their reputation within the community.

- Are they writers?

- Are they speakers?
- Are they thought leaders or a recognized expert and authority in their niche?
- Are they a published author?
- On the flip side, are they someone who has no Internet presence when you Google them?

Generally speaking, people who are up to no good aren't looking for more attention in the form of publicity, speaking, search engine optimization, and book publishing. Those looking to take your money aren't investing their own money into multiple forms of marketing collateral to showcase where they excel to help you. It cuts into their profits!

Who you really want working with you is a recognized expert who is writing, speaking, and publishing in their respective field. Another determining feature of someone you want to hire is seeing if they have referrals from existing professionals. This is one of the best ways to find great advisors. You want to get referrals from people you are already working with and whom you already trust.

A final way to know if you can trust a professional is examining if they have a deep sense of purpose and passion in life. What gets them up every morning? Are they working simply to make more money? Or do they have a sense of divine purpose and a drive to help?

Finding the Best Professionals to Work With

You may be wondering, *Tim, how have you found amazing professionals to work with? Even more importantly, how can you find in-depth professionals to work with?* The first way will be a technical way, just like regular wealth planners do. It's a process to vet the professionals. Next, I'm going to give you the human element way to vet professionals, and this will be the way to spot those highly valuable Elite Wealth Planners.

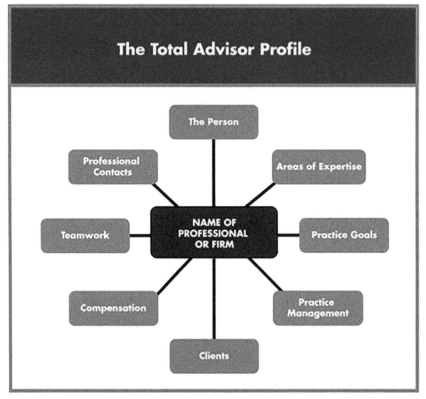

The Total Advisor Profile

Source: CEG Worldwide.   Exhibit 6.4

The First Vetting Process

The Technical Way: Screening Process

One process you can use for finding professions is pretty straightforward and easy: ask other professionals you work with! However, once you get the name of someone, you should always follow up by asking, "Why should I trust this person?" Here are the questions to ask so you can save yourself time, stress—and money.

They have been vetted.

Spend time interviewing potential Elite Wealth Managers. Research their practice. Become familiar with their goals, their objectives, how they do business, and how they calculate their fees. Just as important, you want to know if they have a sense of purpose and passion. There's a lot of people I don't work with because they don't have the technical expertise. They're either not good at what they do, or they kind of rubbed me the wrong way. In other words, I sensed that they didn't have a deep sense of purpose and passion.

They are well-respected in the community.

Most of the people I work with are writers, speakers, publishers, or thought leaders. They are recognized experts in their field and have a very public reputation on the line. In other words, they are not trying to hide. For example, Wes Sierk of Risk Management Advisors is the sixth-largest captive insurance manager in the world. Wes does things the right way, telling potential clients, "There is a line I will never cross because I refuse to put the firm I built at risk. I refuse to push the line past the acceptable point just so you can save a little extra on taxes while my firm gets taken down in the process." Wes has a public reputation as a thought leader and is known for his hardworking, client-centered firm. He will *not* put his firm at risk because he is a man of character, integrity, and prioritizes protecting business owners from the various risks they face.

They have been recommended by trustworthy professionals and have been vetted.

It's all about the vetting process and the referral process. Then it expands into thought leadership. Having a conversation with a potential Elite Wealth Planner will let you know if they are reputable or not.

Some red flags you may not see right away, so it's best to check out the investment professional's background by running a search. You can locate someone's permanent record without crossing any privacy lines because it's public information. Check out: *Brokercheck.finra.org.*

The Dental Wealth Nation™ Vetting Process

When I get into the technical vetting of professionals, not everyone makes it into my Virtual Family Office. Why? Because we have a strict vetting process here at The Dental Wealth Nation™. Let me start by saying that my clients have a thirst for capital to fuel their expansion. I'm always working with different lenders, searching for different lenders, and scoping different avenues for sources—whether it's family offices, SBA experts, or bankers.

I got approached by a gentleman who was eager to become part of my referral system. "Hey Tim!" he said. "I'm a direct lender. I'd like to talk with you about servicing your clients on getting business loans."

"Great, tell me about yourself," I replied. Instantly, he began name-dropping, telling me key people he's worked with, many of whom were significant in the business industry.

"Okay, this sounds good. Let's do a test run," I offered. Soon afterward, I introduced him to a sophisticated client of mine—whom I already had a very good relationship with and would understand what I was doing by testing this lender.

In order to be transparent, I made a disclaimer up front to my client: "This is a new lending contact. I don't know too much about his business approach with client care yet—or his true level of expertise. They claim to work with high-end, significant clients, but have a thorough conversation. Find out what he actually brings to the table of value. In other words, help me vet this person. He's saying some good stuff, but I also feel like there's something lurking under the surface that doesn't feel quite right. From our conversation, he seems like a mover and shaker—a little too concerned about making money, a little too concerned about growing, and not concerned enough to prioritize his clients." Since my instincts can be wrong, I added, "But if he can deliver the whole package, then he'd be a great resource."

However, my intuition turned out to be right. Through the vetting process, I discovered this lender charged a lot of money up front, claiming he'd be able to secure his client a good business loan. Maybe he can; maybe he can't. But what really got me was the barrage of emails he sent: "Hey, when are you going to send me business? When are we going to do a joint webinar? When are you going to give me access to all your clients?" His aggressive approach reveals all sorts of red flags.

I didn't end up working with this lender for obvious reasons. The referral I did make was to another member of my Virtual Family Office, a CPA whom I respect. I wouldn't let an unvetted professional loose on a client. The starting point of my specific vetting process is an interview. If the interview goes well and I intuit that everyone would benefit from a partnership, then I'll do a deeper dive in order to build trust and rapport with them.

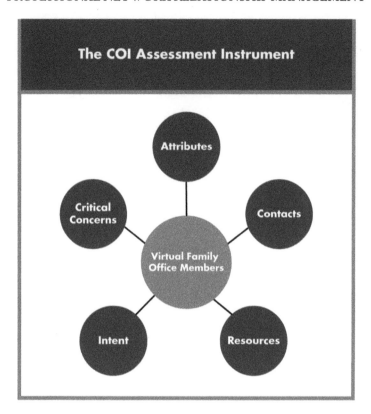

The Professional Advisor Assessment Instrument is a handy visual to help you create a measurable way to determine who should be in your Virtual Family Office. Always ask yourself if they are distinctive in these five categories: attributes, contacts, resources, intent, and critical concerns.

Total Virtual Family Office Profile

When I'm vetting members of my Virtual Family Office, I follow a similar process in vetting my clients. Your goal here is to find the ideal members for your team by asking candidates these key questions:

- What are they like as a person? (Attributes)
- Who do they currently work with? (Contacts)
- What does their financial backing look like? (Resources & Contacts)
- What's their level of expertise? (Attributes)

- How do they manage their business and get paid? (Intent & Resources)

- What are their short-term and long-term business goals? (Intent)

- What are their concerns about working with my team? (Critical Concerns)

- Are they a thought leader within the dental industry? (Attributes & Contacts)

The chart below explains the process I use for vetting advisors. This is how I would approach finding a team for you.

The Advisory Discovery Meeting

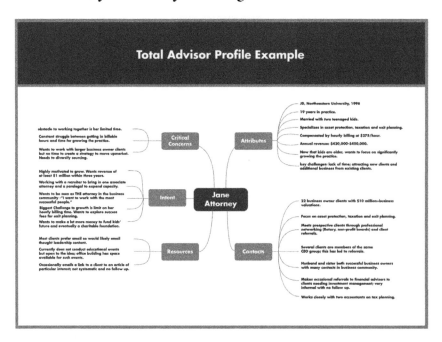

The Second Vetting Process: The Human Element Way

Sometimes it's best to keep things simple and trust your intuition when vetting someone, and it doesn't have to involve research and asking around in the community. There is a tool I use and I want to share with you. This tool will help guide you to gut-check where you are with your different advisors. It's not foolproof, but it's a good way to sharpen your antenna and fine-tune your radar. Start off by mentally reviewing the advisors you're currently working with. They should fall into one of four categories:

- You're disappointed with them. (Disappoint)
- They're delivering what they agreed to deliver. (Deliver)
- You're delighted with them. (Delight)
- They're actively defending you in the midst of an uncertain world. (Defend)

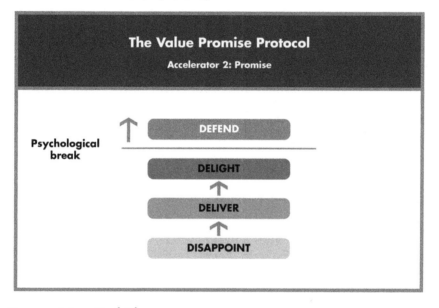

Recognizing Red Flags

On the extreme end, some advisors will straight up disappoint you by not doing what they promised and not returning calls or emails. It eventually becomes a disappointing relationship. Ideally, you need an advisor who is going to deliver, delight, and *defend* you in this chaotic world of uncertainty and challenge you to see a vision that's bigger than you ever thought possible. His goal is to help you thrive. By working with an advisor such as this, he can help you spot warnings in your current professionals that might be red flags. So what are the first steps of vetting people to see if they are displaying red flags?

Step One

Look for recognized authorities within the dental industry who have services or products that you would benefit from.

Step Two

Invite them to an interview to share their knowledge and see how well they serve the audience versus promoting their own products.

Step Three

Do a thorough analysis of their business—the *discovery* process. Then, if their business analysis passes the first test, it's time to move on to the *Advisor Discovery Meeting*. Ask for a video or phone call so you can get to know one another and see if there is synergy between your company and theirs—and if their proposed opportunities will actually serve your clients.

Once you have the person hired, red flags can appear even after they pass the vetting process. Here are some red flags to be aware of to see if you should find another advisor:

Red Flag #1

They are asking you to sign a nondisclosure. I'm not talking about a standard nondisclosure, such as you buying a dental business and wanting to review the financials of another company. Or if you are selling your practice and ask your buyer to not disclose revenue numbers or specific details. These are normal and expected situations where a nondisclosure would show up.

The red flag to be on the lookout for is when the professional says you must sign a nondisclosure and agree not to tell anyone about any of the planning you're doing because it's proprietary—as if there is a secret to hide. The nondisclosure should only apply to the professional not telling anyone about what they're doing with you—not the other way around.

Red Flag #2

They are overly focused on technical wizardry. You'll know this is happening when they try to wow you with big words, going into complicated detail about strategies and tactics. Your response? "Well, that sounds cool, but I really don't understand what it does." Their response? "Yeah, but it's Web 3.0. Trust me!" These business tactics are unhelpful for you. That professional should be able to say, "Well, yeah, we got all this fancy Web 3.0, and HTML, but what it's going to do is create an amazing website to help you communicate clearly to the people, highlighting your values and what you offer. The goal is to build an interactive format that allows you to establish an emotional connection with your audience." Why is the latter response important? You don't care about Web 3.0. You care about what it *does* for you.

Red Flag #3

They are presenting as an Exploiter. Remember from earlier in the chapter that Exploiters are out to benefit themselves. They want to make money, and it's always at your expense; therefore you do not benefit. But they will string you along, making you believe you are on the right track to financial gain. Their words are nothing more than false statements about having "all this money in the future if you only follow me!" and wowing you with their (high-level) technical knowledge. Don't fall into this dreamy state of false security, and do not believe you are receiving excellent client care. Come back to the thought leadership piece, where your advisor is a recognized leader in the community. The stellar professionals you can trust have worked hard to elevate themselves reputably and honorably. You will find people who take the time and effort to build up their authority within a community. These are the pros who actually care about their community and their reputation. They're not going to be making shady deals behind closed doors.

This is where the power of stress testing comes in. If something seems too good to be true, it probably is. Steve Sims, commonly known as the "Real Life Wizard of Oz," often jokes about what it takes to be a consultant these days. He says, "All you need is a picture in front of a rented Ferrari on your favorite social media website with an inspirational quote." What are those images showing? Are they showing people actually involved in everyday life and doing what they're good at? Unfortunately, most Pretenders and Exploiters are like Oz behind the curtain—all talk with no substance.

To sum up, you can use the technical vetting process or the human element vetting process (or both!) to help you discover what kinds of professionals you are working with. When it comes to my specific industry of Wealth Management, there is a hierarchy of where wealth managers fall.

The Advisor Hierarchy

There is a hierarchy within the world of advisors. Specifically, there are advisors who give unqualified advice, investment advisors, financial advisors, wealth managers, and the Virtual Family Office. At the bottom of the hierarchy is where you'll find all the people who like to dole out *unqualified advice.* I'm going to make an assumption that you are not working with professionals who are giving you unqualified advice. There are certainly advisors who have no idea what they're talking about, but chances are you are working with someone who is somewhat capable.

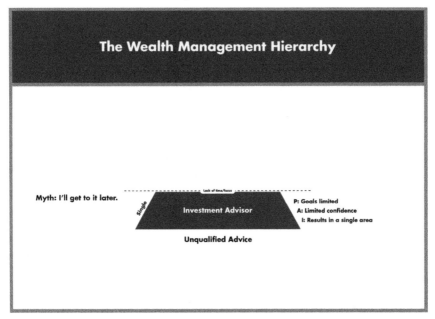

Investment Advisor

Investment advisors represent the first level of the Wealth Management Hierarchy. By definition, they have a singular focus: your investment portfolio. You will eventually have limited confidence that you're going to reach your most important financial goals—or even a few of your smaller ones!

Sometimes, all you think you require is an investment advisor. Unfortunately, many people never move beyond that level because of a lack of time, focus, and *information*. You remain too busy, or so you say, to spend the time making bigger plans for your future. You say, "I will get to it later." That's the myth that we tell ourselves. The truth is that later is always too late, am I right?

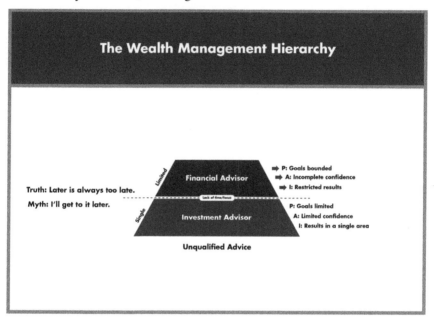

Financial Advisor

Working with a financial advisor will get you some results, but they will be limited. When your needs increase and a heightened level of expertise is needed, they will refer you out to someone else because they are unable to provide the level of service you now want. When the referral is made, it's going to be bound by what you're requesting, which places limits on what you could be doing with your money. A financial advisor will often not be proactive in addressing your financial potential. Sure, they're responsive, but they're not *proactive*. To sum it up: staying with a financial advisor means your goals are going to be bound by what *you've* been able to discover because *you're* having to go to them with ideas. And since you are not an expert in this field, you can't know what you don't know! Only bits and pieces.

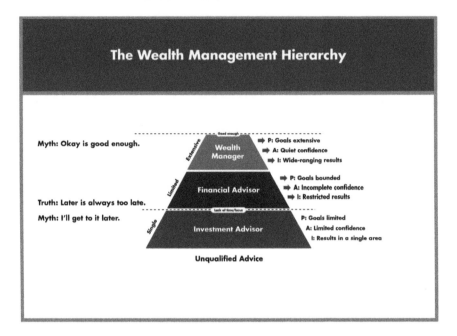

The Wealth Management Hierarchy

Myth: Okay is good enough.

Wealth Manager
- P: Goals extensive
- A: Quiet confidence
- I: Wide-ranging results

Financial Advisor
- P: Goals bounded
- A: Incomplete confidence
- I: Restricted results

Truth: Later is always too late.

Myth: I'll get to it later.

Investment Advisor
P: Goals limited
A: Limited confidence
I: Results in a single area

Unqualified Advice

Wealth Manager

You are definitely making progress on your goals when you are working with someone who has extensive knowledge in many areas, such as the Wealth Manager. Under the care of this expert, you will make extensive progress on your goals. Your Wealth Manager is coming to you with ideas because *they've* done the profiling *for you*. They will be proactive, asking substantial questions to maximize your success, such as, "Based on your situation and what you're trying to achieve, what about implementing 'such and such' strategy? Here's how it can benefit you."

When you have someone who understands your situation and is making proactive recommendations, then you'll enjoy the quiet confidence of being on track as you reach your most important financial goals.

Let's go over the Wealth Management Formula again because it's now in action:

Wealth Management =
Investment Consulting + Advanced Planning + Relationship Management

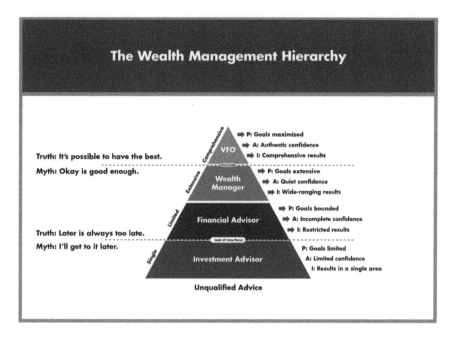

What Five Key Areas Will You See the Most Significant Results?

- **Investment Consulting:** making smart choices with your money

- **Tax Mitigation:** making sure you're never paying too much in taxes

- **Asset Protection:** making sure everything you've worked so hard for is protected from being unjustly taken from lawsuits, divorce, or any unjust means

- **Estate Planning:** taking care of the next generation

- **Charitable Gifting:** impacting causes, and helping out in areas you're passionate about

Virtual Family Office

Yes, it's possible to have the best! When you connect yourself with a Virtual Family Office, you have the opportunity to seize something similar to what the super-rich use to manage their financial affairs. In this hierarchical peak, you're going to receive comprehensive results in all areas of your life, not just financial. One of the best things about a Virtual Family Office is its tailor-made structure. In everything we do, we serve only what's beneficial for you.

If you've seen one Virtual Family Office, then you've seen *one* Virtual Family Office. They are all so different. With me guiding you, I will manage your team of professionals—your CPA, attorney, the accountant, the life insurance specialist, and your retirement planning specialist—and make sure everyone's pulling in the same direction and running cohesively. On an even higher level, I will help manage lifestyle services, concierge medicine, and even private aviation specialists or project managers to help you acquire new property or sell property. You don't have to be involved in any of that. We will build a team of people who can help coordinate your entire life, not just your financial life.

You may have a tax advisor you love. Cool, we'll work with him, but you may realize he's not working very hard for you. You may say, "I don't think my tax attorney knows what he's doing." Great, we'll bring in someone else. If you feel anxious and say, "I don't know if my accountant is doing a good job." Very good. We'll stress test it and find out if we can keep them. If you like him, maybe we just have to do some tweaks with that professional.

Insurance Broker Importance

Very often we outgrow our insurance agent, just like you may outgrow your financial advisor. You started with your local State Farm® or Allstate® agent years ago and don't know where to find the next level of quality service. As life gets more complicated, you will want to move on from these captive insurance agents who work for one singular company and find an insurance broker who can shop the entire marketplace to get you the best coverage, especially for things like cars, boats, and vacation homes.

When you're captive, you're going to have very little flexibility. You're going to get a "state farm" policy from the State Farm® broker.

Captive Manager

My VFO set up a captive insurance company for a doctor who was going to have a huge taxable income that year—higher than it had ever been in his career. I got on the phone with the captive manager and I was talking back and forth with him. All deals have risks—the doctor signing paperwork, warranting and making representations about his financials and everything's in order. Maybe the buyer comes back and finds out something wasn't in order. Honestly, when you're dealing with a lot of numbers, chances are there may be there's a number off here or there. If that's the case, what kind of protection do you have? The captive manager instantly said, "Oh, we can simply add an insurance policy in there for making warranties and representations." And "We can put about 5 percent of the deal size into your own captive insurance company, and on a $20 million transaction, that's $1,000,000 pre-tax dollars."

That's a million dollars that he won't have to pay taxes on, which made the policy effective when he sold the company.

You get the policy ready. Let's say it becomes active when he sells the company, when he signs on the dotted line. Boom, the policy is active, and then he can pay that premium to himself to his own insurance company, to protect against anything in the transaction that may go wrong, or come back on him. That's a huge tax savings. That's the benefit of having a captive insurance company. He's able to insure against risks that he probably couldn't insure against elsewhere.

Super-Rich Rationale for Stress Testing

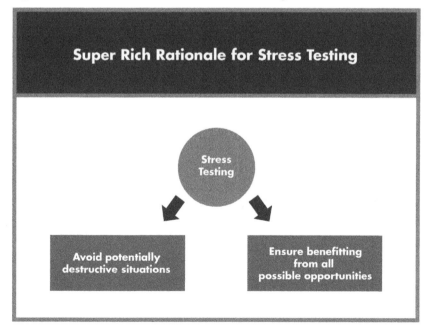

The super-rich stress test their plans, and you should too. The reason the super-rich like to stress test their plans are for two primary reasons. Number one, they want to avoid potentially destructive situations. Number two, they want to ensure they're benefiting from all the possible opportunities.

Visualizing The Stress Test

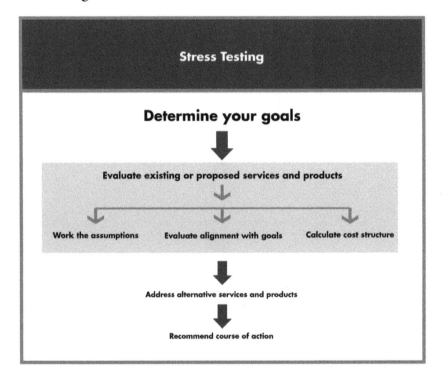

Let's walk through the stress testing process again with all your newly accumulated knowledge.

1. Determine your goals.

2. Look at your existing products and services. What's in place? What do you have? Recall the Virtuous Cycle and see how it fits in here. Remember: the goals represent the profiling piece.

3. It's now time to work the assumptions, then figure out if everything is actively aligning with your goals. Ask yourself, What am I trying to achieve? Then look at

how cost-effective these products and services are while achieving those goals.

4. Look at different services and products. What are the different directions things could go? From there, come up with a recommended course of action.

The Importance of Stress Testing

So often plans change. Life happens and throws our best-laid plans off-kilter: the birth of a child, the death of a family member, a divorce, a new spouse, the acquisition of new assets, and the disposing of other assets. When life changes, your wealth plans change too. Another significant thing to remember is that Wealth Planning so often gets done incrementally. So you met with a financial advisor and got some stuff set up, then you met with an insurance agent and secured some assets. Perhaps years later, you meet with your estate-planning attorney and organize your will. This is a piecemeal strategy where not everything fits together. It definitely contributes to a lack of synergy. Not to mention, you may be overpaying for things because, once again, intentionally coordinated planning was not the path you chose.

Sometimes, things don't work out as planned. Maybe you did work with a Pretender or an Exploiter for a time. But now that you are both wiser and well-informed, you clearly see there are better solutions available to you. How about we look at it from the human element perspective? Maybe you were working with someone who was so focused on technical wizardry that they never achieved what you were hoping to achieve. So that's really once again, kind of the need and the rationale for stress testing.

In a nutshell, stress testing is done for these two key reasons:

- To avoid destructive situations and catch things before they happen.

- To make sure you're taking advantage of financial opportunities you might not know about.

When You're Not 100% Sure...

Implement stress testing to assess your Wealth Planning efficacy in different scenarios and to support the delivery of the expected results.

Courses of Action

Courses of Action	
Course of Action	**Critical Factors**
Stay the course.	The solutions are appropriate
Choose different solutions.	The system has failed.
Choose a different professional.	The solutions are appropriate, but the professionals involved are not truly capable and/or are cost-inefficient.
Modify the approach with the original professional.	A little tweaking is required.
Continue stress testing or get another opinion.	A different professional should conduct the stress test or provide a third opinion.

Common Errors Found When Stress Testing

- Income mitigation strategies were not considered.
- Estate plans do not provide for heirs as desired.
- Excessive amounts of, or poorly structured, life insurance.
- Personal umbrella policies are inadequate.
- Family wealth could easily be lost if children divorce.
- Inheritors are likely to go to war.
- Asset protection plans may have deadly "back doors."
- Charitable monies can easily be redirected

What Should You Do?

At the beginning of this book, you read my origin story, which includes my wife and *why* I do what I do. As we talked about stress testing, I explained briefly about my part in the process. Let me dig a little bit deeper. I'm so passionate about stress testing and love offering it to my clients. I never want another doctor to discover that their plans aren't going to deliver as promised. I never want you to find yourself in a situation and be caught off guard. I want you to thrive no matter what life throws at you. Finding out that your financial plan is not set up correctly is a devastating experience that I hope you never endure.

My approach to stress testing is actually very simple and forms the basis of everything moving forward. It's called *gap analysis*. Gap analysis requires you to always determine where you are now, where you want to go, and then identify the gaps that are in the way of those goals.

What are some common gaps?

- Your investment portfolio is mismanaged.

- Your business isn't optimized, or it is creating undue headaches from lack of efficiency.

- You have an expectation of paying too much in taxes.

- You want to exit your business.

- You want to grow and scale your business.

Then bringing in the right individuals to help you solve those challenges, while having someone who's playing quarterback for you, and orchestrating this entire team so you don't have to. It's pulling all the workload off you for these things. Then that way, you're really the director of your life, and we're serving as a chief financial officer, directing and managing everything behind the scenes for you so you don't have to.

Just like my story—as well as the stories of Dr. VFO, Dr. Exit, Dr. MOC, and Dr. DIY—one of the reasons we've gotten such tremendous results is the continual discovery process. We're always stress-testing and doing scenario thinking. We're always making sure the plans are going to deliver as intended so that we're not caught off guard. On the slim chance we are caught off guard, we've got contingencies for that too.

We're prepared to thrive no matter what life throws at us. I'm known for helping dental professionals thrive in the midst of an uncertain world and, in the process, find more fulfillment and peace of mind than they ever thought possible. I am thankful that's what I'm known for. Knowing that you are leaving a legacy where you have thrived instead of merely survived is a joyous experience.

This is why I do what I do.

If you have an existing VFO or if you have a true Wealth Management Team, then ask them to do stress testing for you because you can't do it by yourself. The reason you can't stress test alone is because *you don't know what you don't know.*

Now that you know the difference between the types of professionals, you must now decide what type of Elite Wealth Planner you want to work with. You've seen the benefits of having your own Virtual Family Office, now I'd like to share with you The Framework for Your Own High-Performing Virtual Family Office.

The Framework for Your High-Performing Virtual Family Office

A high-performing Virtual Family Office is able to integrate Wealth Management with family support services at a level of sophistication that is usually otherwise unavailable to those outside of the already super-rich. That is why you want to analyze your dream team, where you're at, and look in-depth at what's going on, following this framework with the nine core drivers.

How do you actually figure out if you've got some of the best of the best individuals working on your team? The following is a framework you can use whether you've got $10 billion or you've got one dollar in your bank account. It doesn't matter.

If you're working toward your optimal financial world, there are three things that go into it.

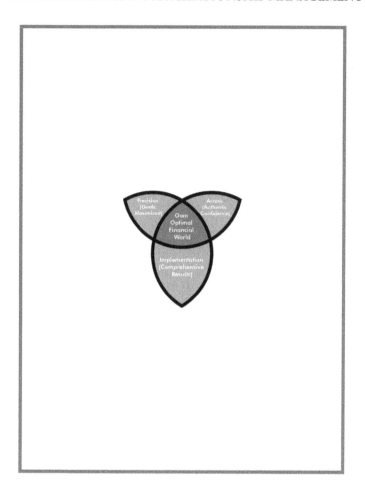

Precision

Precision is about how clear you are on your goals, both business and professional. Clarity matters more than anything else. If you don't know where you're going, you are going to end up who knows where. We want to help you get really clear on your specific goals. This is an area many driven dental entrepreneurs really struggle with. It should be the responsibility of your team to help you always be clarifying your goals and making sure they are maximized.

- Are you working on your goals?
- Are they being maximized?

Implementation

You absolutely require a process that's going to help you reach your goals, and you want an efficient process that's going to help you get there. You also want comprehensive results in all areas of your life. Once again, your coordinator, your Virtual Family Office, needs to take the lead on this to help you implement and navigate the processes that are going to help you reach your goals.

- Do you have clarity about what's important?
- Do you really have authentic confidence that you're going to reach those goals?

Access

Access has to do with your ability and the ability of the professionals you work with. Do you have access to top-of-the-line professionals and state-of-the-art strategies that are going to accelerate you toward the results you want? We have three core elements of the Virtual Family Office.

Precision + Implementation + Access = Success

- How well are these goals getting implemented?
- Are you getting comprehensive results?

First, we start with the human element.

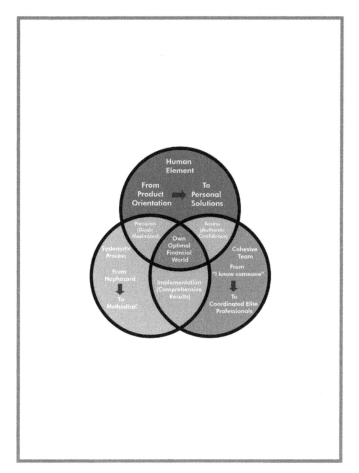

Based on the research from CEG Worldwide, we have discovered that high-performing Virtual Family Offices tend to take specific approaches that are integrated with one another to form a holistic, interconnected framework. There are three major components of the framework:

- **The Human Element:** The ability of your professionals to deeply understand you and your priorities, to communicate with you in ways that enable you to make informed decisions, and to build ever-greater trust and rapport with you.

- **Cohesive Team:** The ability of your professionals to access top-of-the-line specialists, to deliver the most specialized solutions when appropriate, and to provide preferential and cost-effective access to solutions.

- **Systematic Process:** The commitment of your professionals to identify and address mistakes, to find opportunities that may have been overlooked, and to ensure that you are constantly up to date in your approaches.

Human Element

- Are you working with professionals who are product-oriented?
- Have they really moved beyond the products to offering you personal solutions based on your unique circumstance?

Now tie this in with the Virtuous Cycle:

Cohesive Team

- Do you know someone who you're going to refer me to?
- Is it true coordination between team members?

Systematic Process

- What is the process that these professionals are using?
- Is it some haphazard process, or do they really have a systematic, methodical process that they're taking you through to help you reach everything that's important?

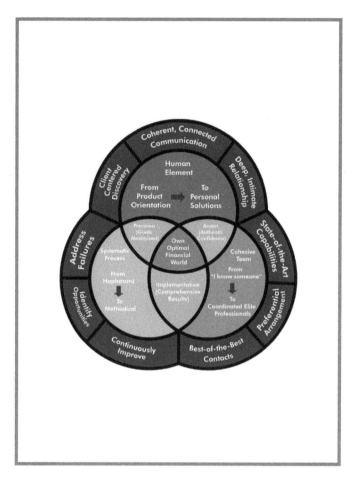

Around each of these elements are three additional core drivers for a total of nine key areas for you to look at. In the human element, there are three areas to examine. Let's examine this chart piece by piece.

Client-Centered Discovery

Do you work with professionals who really know you? Are they asking questions about what's important, or are they just trying to figure out how they can sell you a product?

Coherent, Connected Communication

Do your professionals talk to you in a way that you actually understand what they're recommending? Or do you end phone calls saying to yourself, "I have no idea what they said, but I think it makes sense." Ask yourself: "Do I actually understand what's going on?"

Deep, Intimate Relationships

Do you have personal connections with these advisors? They don't need to be your best friends, but do you have a connection with them that goes beyond just business? Can you continue on with them into a cohesive team with state-of-the-art capabilities?

State-of-the-Art Capabilities

Are you working with the best of the best? If not, can they get access to the best for you?

Preferential Arrangements

This one's huge! Often, when you've got a true coordinated team of elite professionals, you're going to get preferential arrangements, such as jumping to the front of the line. Some of the professionals I work with will not know who you are if you call them at random. They will send your call to voicemail. You might not be getting a call back because they're too busy to talk to you.

How do I do business? Well, I pick up the phone, make an introduction, and say, "Hey, we've got a new client, so you're going to the front of the line. We've got a meeting with these people." You absolutely get the jump in the line. You get preferential access and even negotiated rates with some of these providers because of that cohesive team. Why? Because we're working together, they don't have to do a lot of the same discoveries that they normally would do. We can pass on those savings to you.

Best-of-the-Best Contacts

Is your team made up of the best of the best contacts? Are they absolutely top-tier talent, or are they mediocre? Then, under that systematic process, you move from haphazard to methodical.

Continuously Improve

How does your team continually improve? How are they always working on getting better?

Identify Opportunities

How does your team help you identify opportunities and spot potential areas to get even better?

Address Failures

How does your team address failures? Failures happen. What's the plan when something doesn't go as planned? Now that you know the framework, and we're here together going through it, let's dive even deeper with you. Are you ready?

Red Light, Yellow Light, or Green Light?

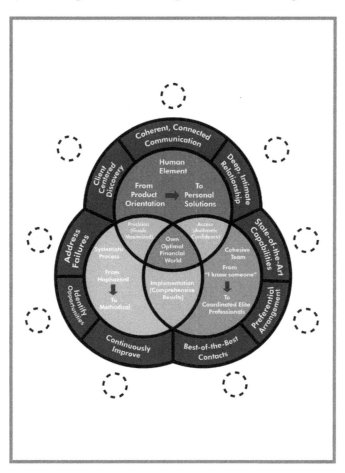

Let's start by visualizing where you're at now. This is a tool I like to call the Family Office Framework, and it's something I use when I conduct live sessions. Look at each of the nine core drivers on the framework in front of you, you'll see little white dots along the perimeter

- *Grab a red, yellow, and green pen* (a marker, colored pencil, or heck, a crayon would work too!).

On a scale of one to ten, rank yourself—*and be honest, this is for your benefit*—on the following categories, starting with the human element section

- **1–3:** If you answered the question with a 1, 2, or 3, you really haven't addressed the issue effectively. Color it red—or put an "R."

- **4–6:** If you answered the question with a 4, 5, or 6, that often means that it's in progress. Color it yellow—or put a "Y."

- **7–10**: If you answered the question with a 7, 8, 9, or 10. This is where you want to be! Color it green—or put a "G."

Where do you fall into each one of these areas? Don't worry, typically, no one has all green on their chart. We've all got room for improvement. Let's get started with the human element section.

Client-Centered Discovery

How well do your current professionals, such as accountants and financial advisors, truly understand you as a person and not just your financial situation?

Coherent, Connected Communication

How well do your current professionals communicate with you on proposed solutions?

Deep, Intimate Relationships

What kinds of personal relationships do you have with your professionals?
Now consider the following three cohesive team questions and answer each one according to its 1–10 scale.

Best-of-the-Best Contacts

How often do your professionals work with the top specialists in fields beyond their own expertise to deliver you the best-available solutions?

Preferential Agreements

How often do your professionals help you "jump the line" when it comes to getting the solutions you need?

State-of-the-Art Capabilities

Do your professionals provide or have access to the deepest expertise and very best solutions available?

You're doing great! Now consider the following three systematic processes questions and answer each according to its 1–10 scale.

Address Failures

Do your professionals use a systematic process to catch and correct any failures and to monitor your situation on an ongoing basis, ensuring that your financial situations are being effectively managed?

Identify Opportunities

Do your professionals frequently employ *What if?* thinking when identifying opportunities and determining the best course forward for you?

Continuous Improvement

Do your professionals evaluate your solutions to determine whether you're on the best possible course or whether an alternative would be more appropriate or effective?

Let's picture your dots colored in on your self-assessment. What would happen if you could turn all those elements green? What if you could take the red ones and the yellow ones and actually have a team of people who are working hard for you? How would your life change? How would your ability to take care of the people you love, and the causes you care about change? Would that make an impact on you? If you could turn them green and do it quickly, is that something you would want to learn about?

You may wonder how do we do this quickly and accelerate your success? I'd like to introduce you to the Four Financial Futures that you face.

The Four Financial Futures

Well, here you are today. Every single one of us is heading toward our certain future financial world. Five years from now, you're going to be there.

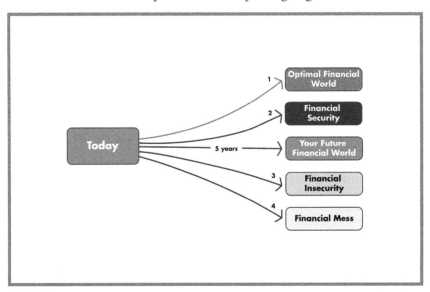

You may be on track toward an optimal financial world, and you're going to hit it because you've got a talented team of people keeping a watchful eye daily on your comprehensive strategy. It always feels good striving for the best and then getting it.

You may be closer toward ending up with financial security—*which isn't horrible*—simply because you took your foot off the gas. Not bad, but not the best. You're happy with your wealth manager. You are drifting toward financial security. You thought, *Okay, that was good enough.* However, the world you started your career in isn't the same as the one you're going to end it in. You forgot to adjust for inflation and unforeseen future expenses. But hey, you were smart enough to get a financial advisor and you did get some results—*just not the ones you had hoped for.*

You might not even be drifting, but worse—you are falling toward a financial mess. You thought you would get to it later, but later is now!

The world changed, inflation killed you, and you weren't protected. But look on the bright side, you didn't upset your investment advisor friend from college. Mark your calendar for your country club tee time this Thursday at nine-thirty—even though you're about to lose your membership. Enjoy it, as it will be your last.

Being Off by Just One Degree

There's a sobering story I'd like to share with you that illustrates how the trajectory you're on today can impact your future dramatically. The unfortunate Mount Erebus Disaster event happened when Air New Zealand Flight 901 took off to go sightseeing over Antarctica from New Zealand on November 28, 1979. When the pilots took off, unbeknownst to them, the navigation system was off by one degree— just one degree. As they got to Antarctica, they descended through the clouds to commence a beautiful sightseeing tour.

As soon as they started descending through the clouds, the pilot screamed, "Pull up! Pull up! Pull up!" In nearly an instant, they had been placed directly on the flight path of a volcano. The plane then crashed into the side of a mountain, tragically killing 237 passengers and 20 crew members. There were zero survivors of the 257 fatalities from the souls on board.

Being off by only one degree cost everyone their lives in that instance.

That was back in the late seventies, and obviously navigation has advanced since then, but when's the last time you checked the direction you're going? This is where you may be heading in your future financial world. If you're off one degree, it can have disastrous consequences down the road. In fact, if you wait too long, you may end up in a situation that's impossible—too costly, too risky, or even harder—to recover from. So the question is: How can you jump those lines—*sooner than later*? How can we move you from drifting toward a financial mess to an Optimal Financial World? How can we do it quickly so you can ride that curve and get the results you want?

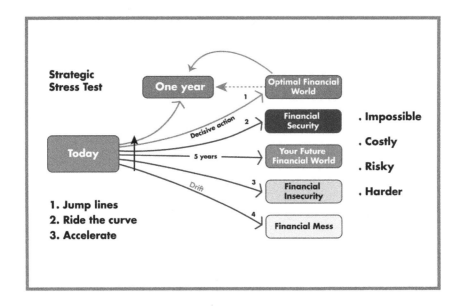

The way you jump those lines is by doing a strategic stress test that can accelerate your results. You can catch those errors and can change the drift, making a tremendous impact on your future by changing just a couple of things today.

By implementing this process, you can jump those lines and reach your optimal financial world a lot quicker than five years from now by significantly speeding up everything.

No matter what you do after reading this book, your future is already happening, and there is nothing you can do to stop time. There is, however, a lot you can do to achieve the outcome you desire.

We can't go back in time, but if we could, I want you to imagine telling the pilots on Flight 901 to take two extra minutes and encourage them to do some stress testing.

- Double-check the navigation system.

- Take a look at the response time of the radars.

- Make sure the flight controls can respond fast enough to correct errors or damage.

- Ask Google or Siri, "What's the weather like today?"

- We're somehow in a time machine, so how about just flat-out telling them, "Seek an alternative route!"

That disaster would have never taken place. But hindsight is always twenty-twenty. Since changing the past is impossible, you can somewhat predict your future. At the time, the pilots didn't know what they didn't know. This is not to bring blame or shame on the pilots; it was a terrible tragedy. The reality is, that we've learned an important lesson that you can apply to your life.

I don't want you to end up on a course heading toward an uncertain financial future. I want you heading toward an optimal financial destiny. Let me share how **you can avoid the disaster.**

Conclusion

I pray by now you're motivated, have a desire to work with a team of the best of the best individuals, and are on track to accelerate your success and thrive. You've seen how the one thing that ties all seven steps of The Wealth Management Process together is *discovery.*

If any of the elements of wealth management take place in a vacuum, they can end up disconnected from your most important goals. If that happens, you will not get the results you want. Wealth Management has to be about what's important to you. The more *you understand yourself,* the better off you, the people you love, and the causes you care about will be. I want to challenge you more than you've ever been challenged, as well as support you more than you've ever been supported, even if you don't work with me. The best way I know how to help support you in doing that is to encourage you to get a stress test done through the discovery process.

Discovery is the *most straightforward* part of the entire process. All it requires is an advisor to be curious about you. It requires an advisor who listens and asks questions. However, discovery is the most neglected step. Most advisors usually ask just enough questions to figure out what is required to make a sale. They never ask any new questions unless there's an opportunity for them to earn more money. This approach stands in stark contrast to a continual, ongoing clarification process, such as the **Dental Wealth Nation Unlimited Discovery™ Process**.

You now have the same seven steps I follow with my clients, but your future rests in your hands. Do you want to implement all seven of these steps and manage every aspect of your team yourself? Do you identify more with Dr. DIY? Or, perhaps you relate more to Dr. VFO and prefer a top-notch team to help you optimize your financial world.

While there are seven key steps, your starting point is just one. It's the **Dental Wealth Nation Unlimited Discovery™ Process** *which includes a complimentary stress test.*

It doesn't take long, and it can literally help you not crash into a mountain. I want to serve you so you can get out there, assemble the best team, work with the best team, and achieve more than you ever thought possible. But to do that, you have to make sure you're on track. Because you are on some kind of trajectory, so let's find out if your current trajectory is a good one or not. Let's find out if you need to do some course correction or not. Wouldn't you like to know?

This is why I have included a special gift for you.

A Gift for You

No matter which character you relate to the most and which of the Four Financial Futures you choose for yourself, I'd like to gift you a complimentary Discovery Meeting that includes stress testing.

Stress testing allows you to dive in and explore your most significant areas of financial concern. You will discover how well your team is performing and better understand if your plans will be delivered as promised.

Even more importantly, you may discover some errors in your planning or, even better, learn additional tactics that can help you. At the very least, we can verify that you are on a solid foundation for moving forward. Then we will make sure you're not missing out on or overlooking any potential opportunities that may be right in front of you.

After reading this book, I want to highlight two takeaways. First, I firmly believe you should **never stop giving.** Second, **you don't need a nine-figure net worth to take advantage of stress testing, discovery, or the Wealth Management Formula.**

Through my Virtual Family Office, I have been able to bring down strategies from the Ultra-Wealthy and make them available to you. Regardless of your financial status, geographic location, or current goals, you can gain access to the top-tier talent of my Virtual Family Office.

Additionally, I've created an entire resource section that highlights the key points we've discussed throughout the book. To access these resources, visit my website: *www.DentalWealthNationBook.com/FreeGift*

Epilogue

T hank you for investing your time with me. It's been an honor to serve you. I hope you've received as much value from this book as I put into writing it—while still keeping it digestible.

I would also like to share one last thing: *Breaking up is hard to do!*

As your wealth and assets grow, it's very common to outgrow your existing advisors.

You may have already received your complimentary stress test, or maybe you're still reading this book and you're planning on doing so afterward. Possibly, you've jumped ahead into the online resources! Either way, you're in a good spot.

We will talk about this during your discovery meeting, but let me begin to ease your mind if it's heavy with these things "you know what you must do" but don't feel prepared to do it yet. Remember that you may need to let some of your current people go, which isn't fun or easy. *Honestly, I hope you don't need to! I simply want to be upfront and transparent so you can continue to move toward success.*

If you do find yourself needing to break up with an advisor, here are the top five ways I've found to be both diplomatic and courteous in the process. You can find more information on this topic in my online resources.

1. Without feeling animosity, make a list of the reasons why the client-advisor relationship has run its course.

2. Thank the previous advisor for their services, and let them know you appreciate the time and advice you've received from them. In other words, show gratitude.

3. Let them know that you want to move in a different direction than you are currently going.

4. The advisor may attempt to make a last-minute effort to keep you as a client. This is to be expected. Remember, you are under no obligation to stay in a situation that you've outgrown. Be firm in your commitment to yourself and to your family.

5. Realize it's in your best interest and in the best interest of your family's legacy to move onward and upward.

Again, I've provided just a handful of tips to help you gain momentum if you need to move on and choose a new advisor. I have additional helpful and motivational tools online. I hope this book has and continues to serve you and your family well for generations to come, so that you can decrease your taxes, increase your impact, and leave your thriving legacy.

God Bless!

About the Author

Tim McNeely is known for helping dental entrepreneurs thrive in the midst of an uncertain world. He is the CEO & Founder The LifeStone Companies and the host of Dental Wealth Nation. Tim serves as the personal CFO to a limited number of successful families helping them take even better care of the people they love, give generously to the causes they care about most, and make a real difference in the world.

Tim is a contributing author to leading dental publications such as Dental Economics, regularly interviewed on top podcasts such as Dentistry Uncensored, and a frequently invited guest speaker to dental industry events. In addition, Tim is the host of the top-rated "Dental Wealth Nation" show where he interviews top dental thought leaders. In Tim's bestselling book, Dental Wealth Nation, Tim is committed to helping you thrive even more.

However, what matters most to Tim is meeting his wife, Dr. Dana Yeoman.

Seeing his wife's frustration with the complexity of running a dental practice, he saw that he could have a big impact on Dana's business, so he set out to make things simple.

Since meeting Dana, Tim has helped many dental entrepreneurs Optimize their Financial World even more so that they can decrease taxes, increase impact, and leave their thriving legacy!

He does this by sharing strategies from the Super Rich (Net Worth of $500 million or more) and making these strategies available to all dental entrepreneurs, no matter what their net worth.

Tim and Dana enjoy California's wine country, savoring a good single malt, raising standard poodles, and supporting world missions.

Thank You

I am always striving to ensure my books offer unparalleled information on the topic I'm spotlighting. My goal is to provide you with the tools you are seeking to best serve your needs—and your family's needs—as you navigate this industry. And one of the ways I achieve this is through your feedback.

My ask: Please leave me an honest review on Amazon and Audible, depending on how you purchased the book, so I can read your feedback, fine-tune my communication for the next book, and get a feel for what you loved most and found useful in your life. In advance, I'm offering a heartfelt "Thank You" for your time and honesty.

www.DentalWealthNationBook.com/Review

Writing a review also makes a significant impact on the potential readers who are choosing which book might be of most use to them among the dozens out there. And if you are anything like me, a driven entrepreneur, I want to select a book with great reviews that explain why readers found it not just helpful, but life-changing!

You likely don't know me from Adam, but hopefully you read some reviews, previewed the book, decided to invest, and found my information beneficial, which then inspired you to set up your own Virtual Family Office. I would still, of course, ask you to leave a review so I have your feedback and can keep improving.

So what do you say?

Would you be willing to leave me a quick review in order to help dental entrepreneurs everywhere decrease their taxes, increase their impact, and leave their thriving legacy?

~ Tim

Ingram Content Group UK Ltd.
Milton Keynes UK
UKHW050649060623
422904UK00008B/254/J